Jeff Cop

Jack Fleeman

ISBN 978-1-64003-413-6 (Hard Cover)
ISBN 978-1-64003-414-3 (Digital)

Covenant Books, Inc.
11661 Hwy 707
Murrells Inlet, SC 29576
www.covenantbooks.com

Dedication

The author dedicates his book to his children, "Emily, Sara, Gabi, Jon, and Max, this book is for you. This might help explain, that while following my dream, why I may have missed a celebration or two, perhaps a holiday, or just away from home too often."

If you ever had a really great time, perhaps a great vacation, a great family visit, a fantastic time with some friends, or any other time that you can look back on and smile with the memories, well, that is how I can look back at my thirty-six-year career as a police officer.

I have been retired a few years now, and I can fondly look back at a lot of hard work, a lot of good times, some not so good times, and just overall reflect back to my career and know how lucky I have been. I surely hit a few "speed bumps" in my career, but I always tried to keep my chin up and keep a positive outlook. To attempt to compare my career to a great family vacation would be to try to learn from a problem on vacation and not let the flat tire, mistake in a reservation, or even a sudden change of plans keep me from making the best of things.

I think a lot of people sometimes look at me with surprise or maybe even suspicion because I can remember so much about my career and the events within it. I may not remember all the names of all with whom I crossed paths, but I certainly recall the events and lessons I learned.

Since I retired, I have given much thought about what made me think what I did was so special. I always felt that the journey was a big lesson in life. My experiences in police work always seemed to be a learning ground for the future. Learn from everything I was doing, and I did try to impress that on those with whom I worked.

I doubt that very many police officers that I worked with looked at the position as anything more than a good job. Some did the job a whole lot better than some of the other ones, and some probably should never had been a police officer.

I never thought of myself as a wizard of police work, but I did try to learn from all aspects. And I did learn a lot. And now, it's over. I am friends with many of the officers I worked with, whether they worked at the same departments as I did, or we had chances to work together somewhere along the road.

I worry about the officers who work the job in these days, and I have to sit back and watch as our world changes before my eyes. I usually don't get very close to any actual police situations and just watch events unfold on television like most folks do.

I don't have any ideas whether or not any other police officers write about their experiences, but I felt compelled to share what I learned.

Perhaps a young person who is playing with a remote notion to someday try to be an officer will read my stories. I know if my mother was still on earth, she would probably read a little bit from this book every day. At the least, people who worked and lived in the places I worked may have an interest in getting a glimpse from another angle of something that happened near them.

I was never an honor student in school, but of all the books I had to read for book reports, this book would have caught my fancy.

I will start at the beginning when I was a child, and I will try to demonstrate where I came from, both in a physical sense and what was in my mind to aim at the career I followed.

It was just after supper, and a man came by the house to take my dad somewhere. Dad didn't go to many places without Mom, especially in the evenings. I stayed in my bedroom and listened to Dad, and the man talk with Mom, and then I heard Dad leave. I went right out to the living room and asked my mom where Dad went. She told me he was getting a job as a policeman and had to go to a meeting about the job. This was the evening that changed my life.

This was in May 1955, and I was born in November of 1951. I have always wondered how I remembered so much detail at that young age, but this has always been something I have always had the ability to do during much of my life. I was almost four years old, and my dad was going to become a policeman! I have always wondered what all the influences were that I was under at that age to know my dad was going to be a hero.

I went back to my room that evening and went to sleep. I shared a bedroom with my brother Steve. My brother was two years older than I was, and I remember he never seemed to be very interested in where Dad had went. I kept to myself when I went to sleep that evening, keeping a keen ear for the rattle of the front door knob. I could always tell by that rattle if someone was coming in the front door. That was always Mom or Dad. Dad told me years later that he came home after 2:00 a.m. I had no clue what time it was when I heard him come in. I heard the doorknob rattle, and after a few quiet moments, I heard him open the hall closet door. I jumped from bed and went straight out into our living room to see Dad. I asked him if it was true that he was a policeman, and I cannot explain the thrill I had when he told me yes. He was a Jeffersonville policeman. Dad walked over to the hall closet (where I had heard him open the door), and he showed me police uniforms hanging in the closet. It was at that point Dad told me I needed to go back to bed, and I think that was one of the best night's sleep I can remember. I never realized it then, but many years later, I would understand that, that was one of the very best evenings of my life.

The next day, Dad had gone to work at his regular job at the Quartermaster Depot where he worked as a painter. As I was alone in the house, I opened the closet where his uniforms hung and stood there admiring them. The police patches on the sleeves were surreal. I was so deeply impressed that I knew at that young age I wanted to be a policeman too. I always figured all kids wanted that, but I lived with my dad, a policeman, and I knew that this was what I wanted to be. This never changed.

It may have been my upbringing, or just me being myself, but I was satisfied I was going to be a policeman just like my father was.

I grew up watching things go along in life in Jeffersonville. We had a big backyard, and there was plenty of room to play. My grandpa and grandma lived close by. They were a big part of our family. They were my dad's parents. My mother's parents came from Russia and lived in Michigan. Mom had met Dad when he got out of the navy at the end of World War II. They came to live in Dad's hometown.

Growing up, I always felt somewhat special because Dad was a city policeman. He was important. In grade school, my principal, Mr. Moss, always talked to me about my parents, and I always believed it was because Dad was a policeman. Looking back, Arthur Moss was an excellent educator and always a friend. He probably treated all the students alike. He surely did. But he sure made me feel special. He set an example that has forever been in my mind of what a leader should be like and how to be good to those you worked with. He was well-liked by other students, and all the teachers seemed to really respect him as well.

In the fourth grade at Ingramville Elementary School, I was in Miss Lytal's class. She agreed with Mr. Moss that I should be a member of the school's crossing guard. I never felt as proud as when they told me I could help as a crossing guard. Normally, you had to be fifth-grader. But I knew they selected me because my dad was a policeman, and I was therefore qualified for the job. I wore a white belt across my chest with a badge on it. It was a silver badge, but there were gold ones for captains. We wore white helmets and carried a long cane pole with a red flag at the end of it. (I had already set my goal to wear the gold lieutenant's badge someday.) In the meantime, in the mornings and afternoons, I was always ready to be at school at the right time for me to put on my gear and accompany my "squad" to whatever street I was assigned to be a crossing guard. That was only Eighth Street (in front of my house) or Tenth Street, which was just a light-traffic street. Today, a policeman with lights and sirens on would have trouble stopping cars to let kids cross on either of those streets!

I grew up playing GRC Little League. I played the Saturday Morning League and the "farm" league. I never made it to the "senior" league. My dad only made one game during my little league career. He and Mom were both there that memorable evening when I did hit my one and only career home run. I even sent the ball over the center field sign that Cottonwood's Sporting Goods sponsored. I won a free baseball bat because of that sign! More than anything, I enjoyed the summer practices and afterward getting a cold bottle of soft drink from a nearby store.

My childhood was great. If I missed anything, I didn't realize it. Dad didn't make much money, and Mom went to work at Bacon's Department Store. She always worked long hours in the business office. The store was at Youngstown Shopping Center, which was new at the time.

That shopping center and the fact that my mother worked there so long did have somewhat of an impact on my upbringing.

Dad worked a different shift every month. It seemed that most of the time we had to be quiet because he was sleeping.

Mom seemed to work a lot. I enjoyed visiting her at the store's credit office. That office handled layaways, gift wrapping, customer's charge accounts, and that is where the store's switchboard was at. When they weren't too busy, she'd let me plug the wires in the store's switchboard. I never did really understand how those things worked. I pretty well had a free run of the store. I questioned Mom why the store had a restroom near a storeroom that had a hand-printed sign reading "colored only." I knew what it meant and knew it wasn't right. Many of my friends were *colored*, and she understood my questioning.

During my grade school and junior high school years, I did something with my group of buddies that still amazes me that we were ever able to accomplish. We made monster and science fiction-type movies. One of my friends, Rick Pruitt, was probably the best read student of science fiction films. Rick had a file box full of cards for just about any science fiction and horror movie made. Plus, my brother loved science fiction and another friend of his was into art. With their direction, artwork, and acting, and with several more of us working as *actors*, we made a remake of Frankenstein. We tried to remake Dracula a couple of times, but the movie always turned into something else. We used real theater makeup, bought 8mm film with our allowances, rented an airplane ride to get some aerial films for a spaceship scene, and improvised costumes using school play costumes. We recouped some of our expenses when we charged admission to let our friends watch the finished movies. It was fun at first, but eventually this film business became real work. Plus, it was hard enough to take orders at home from my older brother and then again when he "directed" me and criticized my acting. It seemed every Saturday morning I found myself on the bus to Louisville to the store where we bought our movie film and had it processed. There were about ten of us who participated in making these movies. I always felt we all enjoyed it, and we knew we were special for just doing it. I never knew anyone else our age who even tried to do it to the scale we did it. We had the camera, floodlights, someone's basement or garage, makeup, props, and along with the knowledge of what we wanted to show and the intent to get it done, we accomplished quite a bit.

We all eventually outgrew this movie thing; however, a couple of the guys went on to really act. I've seen them in movies and commercials on television. I think Rick still does acting in New York.

I went all through school without getting into any trouble, nothing at all. My friends in school always told me I didn't get into trouble because my dad was a Jeff cop. That wasn't true. If they only knew the truth. My dad would have beat my butt if I did anything wrong. Dad always told me that if I did anything wrong, he'd tell "Judge Clem" to send me to boy's school. Later in life, I learned that Judge Clem wasn't really a judge, but a probation officer. He probably could have sent me to the gallows back then if he'd seen it to be the fitting punishment. No, my friends were really wrong. I had a lot of good reasons to not get caught doing anything. Getting caught was the big word.

You know, I paid more attention to what my dad did than he ever knew. I'm talking about when he worked. He may have thought I was just friendly when he came home from work in the early afternoons or late evenings, and I stayed in his bedroom while he changed clothes. There is no telling how many times I lay across his bed while he changed out of his police uniform and we talked. I always asked him how his day went and what he did. He learned that when I asked those questions, I wanted to hear details of all the calls. I didn't care if he was working radio and sending police to calls or if he was responding himself. I always asked for details and why he did this and why he did that. I never asked why he didn't do this or why he didn't do that. That's because I was trying to learn to be a Jeff cop. I never, ever, told anyone about these conversations, and even Dad didn't ask why I was so inquisitive. I knew he thought I was just real interested in his job. Later I would appreciate that why he almost welcomed my questioning, and he never cut me off or refused to answer my many questions. It was like he enjoyed talking about things. Today, when something pretty traumatic has happened, we have people who are trained to talk with officers. This helps relieve the trauma to our souls. Those moments when Dad had just gotten off work were probably the only moments we discussed what he did on the job.

One morning, I can remember his running home while on duty and changing clothes into civvies, only to return home a few minutes later to put his uniform back on. It was one of those times that he told me that a dangerous fugitive was in a drug store downtown, and

11

they were going to catch him. But he had gotten caught before Dad could get there. Dad was so disappointed.

One morning, I was getting ready for school, and my mom told me to be really quiet and not to awake my dad because he had a bad night. Dad was working the night shift. My mother was visibly shaken. I asked what was wrong, and she explained that at some apartments less than a block from where we lived, a man had strangled his eight-year-old nephew to death. The boy was spending the night, and the uncle had just had his feet removed from a frostbite injury, and the kid was jumping up and down on the end of the bed, on his uncle's stubs. And after being told to quit many times, the uncle killed his nephew. I never heard another word about that. I always thought I would hear who the kid was but never did. To this day, I think about it every time I pass that apartment building.

I never cared what the situation was. If Dad said someone had called the police about a neighbor's dog barking too much, I would ask, "What did you do, why, and what did they say?" He always explained in full detail to me what he did. I felt I was always in training for my future career. I found myself always asking Dad what did you do and why. There obviously wasn't a science to what the police did but rather acting on past experiences. He explained that sometimes you can tell somebody something, and there are some people who you cannot tell anything to.

Taking Aim at a Career

As I got older, I found myself getting more serious about my career choice. I wanted to be a Jeffersonville Police Officer. I wouldn't need a college degree to get hired, not that I thought I shouldn't attain a degree, but I knew how to aim at the job. My brother, Steve, had graduated from Jeffersonville High School in 1967. He was always an electronics whiz. He applied at Purdue, and I will never forget my mother taking me aside one day to discuss college. Mom told me Steve had been accepted by Purdue University, and she asked how I felt if I knew she and Dad could not afford to send us both to college. I appreciated that moment in my life. I told Mom that I planned on being a Jeff cop, and I didn't need a degree. I told her I did want to go to college and wanted to attend Indiana University Southeast, and I would pay for it myself. The school was close by and that's what I wanted to do. Everything went good after that. Steve went to Purdue. He majored in electronics engineering.

Steve moved out and went to Purdue. We would drive up to West Lafayette and visit him often on weekends. He and I both had played in the Jeffersonville high school band and after high school, he went on to play in the Purdue marching band. He sent us a post-card once showing a diagram of a routine the Purdue band would be performing at the Minnesota football game, and he circled where he would be positioned. I'll never forget that game. The game was on national TV and during the halftime show, Mom and I looked for Steve. We saw his small figure and his trombone slide going back and forth and knew it was him, right where he said we'd be able to see him. He was about the size of an ant though. It wasn't exactly a moment of fame for him, just the band. The band was great.

He had told me several times the story about how he was late to get on the band's bus one day during final exams. The Purdue band was going to perform in the Indianapolis 500 Parade. By the time Steve ran up to the bus, the band director had already replaced his position in the parade. Steve told me how he had ran from the classroom to catch up with the rest of the band. The band director assigned Steve to be one of the other band members to carry the band's banner in front of the band during the parade instead. That just happened to be the year Paul Newman was filming a movie about the 500, and Steve was filmed carrying the banner. Anytime that movie is on television, I watch it until I get that split-second glimpse of Steve carrying that banner in front of the band.

Steve moved on and after graduation taught at Purdue and then at a college in Rockford, Illinois, where he also worked for an aerospace company. He worked on a lot of the electronics for the space shuttle. He would sometimes call me whenever a shuttle launch was postponed due to some glitch. His team was always worried the delay was because of one of their systems failing. He was relieved when it was determined that something else caused the shuttle's problem, and it wasn't something they had worked on. He had helped redesign some of the systems of the shuttle after the Challenger exploded.

Steve went on to write a college electronics textbook, *Electronic Devices*. He also taught for many years. I have always been proud of his accomplishments.

In the early years after high school, Steve would sometimes ask me why I stayed in Jeffersonville. He said there were so many opportunities out there, and I should leave town. I probably responded in such a way that I offended him. But why would I leave town? I want to be a police officer here, and besides, this is where our family is.

After a few of those discussions, we never talked about it again.

I graduated from Jeffersonville High School in 1969. I had always been a mediocre student. I don't remember many nights when I ever stayed home to study. I thought studying meant getting your homework done. I did do that. Later, I found out what studying meant. I had trouble when I went to college and needed to study.

I was accepted at Indiana University Southeast. The campus was located here in Jeffersonville at the time. It was a very crowded campus. The Vietnam War was in full force, and when I turned eighteen, I went to the Census Bureau here in town to register for the draft. The draft board had a small office there. I had to re-register a couple of times. I remember the woman who ran the office was always being so compassionate when I came in. She seemed know every young man in town. We all knew her. That draft card she gave us each to carry was supposed to be in our possession at all times. That's probably part of the reason all of us draft age guys knew that woman. Her name was on all of our cards. Not being drafted was very important to all of us. Anyone I had known who had been drafted came home in a coffin.

One day, my dad told me that a close friend of his, who was an FBI agent, had told him that if I had the interest, I could apply for a clerk's job with the Louisville FBI office, and this agent told Dad that once I was hired, he could get me transferred as a clerk for the FBI at the New Albany office. They didn't have anyone working in that office except agents at that time. I thought this was outstanding. I knew I would never be considered for a job as an FBI agent without a college degree. I knew that if I got hired as a clerk, I'd at least have my foot in the door towards an agent's position. Dad's FBI friend's son had worked as a clerk for the FBI and was just hired as an agent. I applied right away. It was about a month before I got a call from them. This FBI agent called me in for a Saturday morning interview. I was so pumped up. I knew that once they got to know me, they'd hire me.

When I went for the interview, things went south really fast. The agent who interviewed me got right to the point. You see, on one part of the application, I was asked if I had relatives in any foreign countries. I told the truth and said yes. The application asked me to state which country, and I told the truth. Russia. My maternal grandparents emigrated from Russia, and our family always spoke about relatives who remained there. I never knew their names, but

I surely have a lot of family there to this day. This was about 1971 when I applied. You have to keep in mind what the political situation was between the United States and Russia. I knew I would never have a problem being a good citizen and FBI employee, but this agent who interviewed me cut me off short. He told me there was absolutely no way I would be hired. He said anyone having relatives in a Communist nation were security risks, and the FBI would regard me as a risk. I sat in that small room feeling crushed. I didn't know what else to say. I never had any thought that the world of politics would keep me out of any job. But my pride with my family quickly overrode that feeling, and I was actually trying to find an excuse to escape from this interview. I knew what was right and wrong, and they were wrong with this one.

To add to my pain, the agent immediately tried to recruit me as an informant for the FBI. I have always felt that was more important to the FBI than for them getting me as an employee. He told me that Indiana University was a hotbed for domestic terrorism, and I was in a good position to gather information. I knew what he meant. There were always news stories about these radical groups, and their fugitive bomber associates secretly met on Brown County farms near Bloomington. I knew some students I went to IUS with attended antiwar rallies, and some drove to Washington, DC, to march. This agent seemed very dutiful while I observed him. He was just doing his job. But at one point, he suggested I think about recruiting informants on behalf of the FBI, and I really became mad. I felt so insulted and disillusioned when I left the FBI office that morning. But you know, it wasn't too long after that, that I did understand what had happened to me. I felt I was a qualified applicant for this job, and this agent may have realized this but told me the absolute truth that I'd never get hired. But I also felt he knew I had good intentions, and he took a chance to recruit me to be a snitch. I knew not to ever say anything about those agents my father knew and had told me to apply for this job. But I did think that they may have had a "heads up" who I was. That didn't happen at all. I knew this was another lesson for me to learn. I was young, and I was learning things all the time, and I knew I would find many things out and sometimes find them out the hard way.

I attended IUS full-time which qualified me for a 2S student deferment. That was draft board classification for full-time students making those with that classification ineligible for the draft. I always felt a little guilty for not allowing myself to be drafted. But anyone I knew from town that went to the war came back in a coffin. While I was living at home, on that student deferment, I will always remember seeing Richard "Pony" Leavell walking past my house every Sunday morning, carrying a brown paper sack. He had been a basketball star at Jeffersonville High School. I loved our team and loved to watch them play. I sometimes dreamed the Jeff team would become state champions. Leavell was one of the players I always loved to watch play. He and I never knew each other, but I admired his basketball ability, and I respected him for being a good person.

I was living at my home on East Eighth Street when it seemed every Sunday morning I could see Richard "Pony" Leavell walk past my house. He always walked taking long strides with those long legs getting him wherever he was headed, quicker than most people. I always wondered where he might be going. He was always carrying a brown paper sack, which I knew was his lunch. I never had a clue where he was headed until one Sunday afternoon when I happened to drive past a doctor's office in Youngstown Shopping Center and saw Pony sitting on the curb outside eating his lunch from the paper sack. I could see that he was cleaning that office. Now I knew where he was going. I never saw him walk past my house after that day. A few months later, I read his name in the paper. He had been sent to Vietnam and had been killed in the war. He was just another person who stuck in my mind. This happened with a lot of people and situations. I drew from everything, good and bad, and molded my mind and I guess my personality by the things I observed. I hadn't ever been told otherwise. I just watched and learned. Many years later, a close firefighter friend of mine, Dale Richardson, was being buried, and I looked around at the other gravestones during the graveside service. Dale was being buried next to Richard Leavell. I had never seen Pony's grave before that. My friend Dale Richardson wouldn't have planned his burial any better. Dale and I had attended high school together, but we didn't become friends until years later. He was a ranking fireman, and he and I drank several beers together talking about our lives and how we looked at things until one day I learned he had died at home. Even more years after that, I took a photo of Richard Leavell's name at the Vietnam War Memorial wall in Washington, DC. I gave a copy to one of his cousins when I returned home.

During college, I worked at Bacon's Department Store on weekends. Friday afternoons, I made signs with a small printing press and cleaned the store on Saturday mornings. I later worked at Belknap's Hardware in Louisville during the summer. I loaded trucks and worked on the shipping floor. A friend who owned a security company also hired me to guard a local quarry on weekends to keep vandals out.

I had finished my third year at IUS, and everything in my life seemed to be going so great. It was a feeling I had never experienced. I was looking toward getting finished with college and then joining the police department. The thought of how good it felt was on my mind night and day. For at least for a week or so anyway. This was a feeling that I have learned to be suspect. You always hear about people having a "sixth sense," deja vu, and whatever else that seems to tell you in your mind that something is going on, and you may not know exactly what it is. Years later, I would have that same feeling again.

I was preparing to go to one of my friend's graduation party one evening, and when I arrived home, I found all of Dad's clothes in the garage. Mom told me what had happened between them, and she was making him leave.

My mother had always been a meek person, and in one way, I was glad she realized things about my dad, but their marriage and that great feeling I was experiencing about my life being so great was crashing quickly. I did go to the party. After a short time there, a neighbor called on behalf of Mom, telling me I needed to come home. Things went very badly when I arrived. It was so bad that I called the Jeffersonville Police. They did arrive and spoke with Dad and Mom. They recommended Mom and I find a place to stay. We left.

Mom went to Michigan and stayed with her family. Dad moved out of the house and got an apartment. I stayed in the house and packed everything because Mom had put the house up for sale. I worked nights for a security company monitoring burglar alarms and tried to keep going to school. My grades suffered, and IUS wouldn't let me attend school full-time. I lost that deferment from the draft. I lived on edge for only six months, and then the government started a lottery system for the draft. My number was high, and they said I wouldn't be drafted.

I quit the security company and went to work as an orderly at a hospital in Louisville.

I felt stronger than ever to become a police officer now. I quit college and worked full-time at the hospital. Mom had returned to town and got herself an apartment in Louisville. I lived there with her for a few months.

While at the hospital, I met Carla Fox. She was a student nurse there at the hospital. We dated constantly, and five months later, we married. That was May 1973. We moved into an apartment in Jeffersonville, and she worked as a registered nurse at the hospital, and I worked as an orderly and eventually became a supervisor in the unit management department. I supervised dozens of girls who worked at the hospital as unit secretaries, couriers, and transcribers. I hated that job.

I went to the Jeffersonville Police Department and asked Chief Raymond Parker if I could get a job. The chief told me they had no openings, and besides that, he didn't know how that would work with my father working there. Dad never knew I went there. We hardly spoke. A lot of things happened during the breakup with Mom, and that's just the way it played out.

After Chief Parker turned me down, I went next door to the Clark County Sheriff's office. Sheriff Gilbert and I knew each other well. His son Johnny and I had been close friends in high school. The sheriff's quarters were adjacent to the jail, and I used to go by Johnny's house, and we'd each get a big thick-sliced piece of bologna and make ourselves a sandwich. Those were good memories.

Sheriff Gilbert looked me in the eye when I asked him for a job and told me I didn't want to work there. I took him for his word. He would never steer me wrong. Woody Gilbert was a fine man, and I always looked up to him as a respectful law enforcement officer.

So I applied with the Indiana State Police. I knew I had what it takes to join that department, but two things bothered me. My vision was awful, and I wore contacts. The state police had high physical requirements, and I really didn't think they'd let me on, but I tried them twice. The second thing that bothered me about joining the state police was that if I was hired, I knew I'd have to move away. I wanted to stay close to home where my family lived. The same reason I didn't listen to my brother when he suggested I leave town.

The first time I applied with the state police, I never heard anything. They were having a big push toward hiring blacks, and I was told by a friend that I wouldn't have a chance, at least for now.

The second time I applied, I received a letter telling me I scored sufficiently on the written exam, and I would be progressing through the hiring process.

One morning, while alone in our apartment, I heard a knock on the door. At the door was an Indiana State Police detective. I knew who this detective was. He was one of the sharpest investigators I had ever known about. Well, I was hoping my vision wouldn't be considered so quickly in this process, but it was and understandably so. When the detective arrived, he found me in a rare moment when I was wearing my thick-lensed glasses. Vanity kept me in my contact lenses almost all the time. I didn't have them on that morning, and he asked me what my vision was. I really didn't know the numbers, but I was "off the chart" nearsighted. I gave him my optometrist's name and address.

I wanted terribly to call the optometrist's office and beg them to do something so not to make me look bad. But I knew better, and I didn't make the call. Days later, I did speak with the lady in the doctor's office. I asked her if the detective had come by. She said yes. I asked her what she had told him. She replied, "I told him the truth, you're as blind as a bat."

I was feeling so frustrated. I knew I needed patience to find a job. I really didn't want to work for the police department except for the Jeffersonville Police, but I needed to do something. I was married, my wife was making more than twice than I was making, and I had assured her I was going to be a police officer.

It wasn't long until I gave some thought about applying for something in police work other than conventional policing. When I was underage, I would go with friends to a pizza parlor in Louisville and drink pitchers of beer. I had always been big and looked old enough and never had a problem getting served. I remembered one Sunday evening, I went into this pizza parlor, and the ABC men were sitting at a table. These guys were in suits with their police radios setting on their table in front of them. I was brazen enough back then to go ahead and order a pitcher of beer. When my regular waitress, Rose, told me she'd have to see my ID because the ABC was there, I told her I felt insulted since I had been coming in for such a long time. She agreed with me, and I drank my beer with my friends (who were old enough).

I sent a letter to the Indiana Alcoholic Beverage Commission at Indianapolis asking them if they had police positions in their department and mentioned I might be interested in such a position. A few days later, I received a big envelope from them. It was an application for the Indiana State Excise Police. I had never heard of them. The application was identical to the Indiana State Police application. I filled it out and sent it back.

Only a few days went by, and I received a phone call from an excise officer wanting to meet me at my home for an interview.

Two days later, Officer Charlie Neideffer and Officer Rieke Meyer came to my apartment. They both worked at the district office at Madison, Indiana, about forty-five minutes away from Jeffersonville. They asked me if I would be willing to work in my home district, meaning I wouldn't need to move. Of course, I said yes. They told me they would get back with me, and they left. A few days later, I received a form for a physical and a letter telling me to get a doctor to fill out the form and get it back to them soon. I went to the hospital where I worked and a doctor there gave me the physical and I sent it the form back.

Another few days passed, and I received a letter from the excise police. I was hired and needed to report to the State Office Building in Indianapolis on May 28, 1974, to begin a two-week recruit school. I was very excited about getting hired, but a slight bit apprehensive about the quick process.

This was the beginning of my law enforcement career.

My Experiences Working for the Indiana State Excise Police

I promptly reported that May morning. The excise police head-quarters was also adjacent to the Indianapolis District office. There was the chief, Phil Sanders, a really robust man; his assistant, Major Ross Portolese; and I met Lieutenant Lautzenhizer. He was in charge of training and would be my instructor for the recruit school. The department had two captains: one for the north part of the state, and one for the south part. They normally were "out in the field." The first time I heard that term, I pictured them out near some corn. Sgt. Pete Weiss worked in headquarters also. Pete was a good guy. I never knew exactly what he did other than helping out at headquarters.

I was so warmly received by all of those officers. Probably the biggest friend I made there was the chief's secretary, Joann. She did just about all the clerical work, typed all of our reports, and always had the answers you needed.

The recruit school would start right away in the State Office Building. Attending the school were several new hires like me from different parts of the state.

There were some more officers who attended, but they had been working for some time. This was the department's first recruit school. From what I learned, in years past, the department consisted of mostly political hires, many of whom were former police officers, and a new approach had been taken to make the department better trained, more professional, and with more officers. It seemed I fell into this just at the right time.

The recruit school was conducted in the lower level of the building in a partitioned section of the State Office Building cafeteria. It was a pretty quiet place and handy when it came time for lunch. It seemed just about all state employees who worked in the building came there at one time or another.

My new job was a plainclothes job. I would be working in a district office, conduct periodic inspections of locations with alcoholic beverage permits, investigate complaints of violations of the Indiana Alcoholic Beverage Laws, Rules, and Regulations. I would be conducting raids at permit locations, at bootlegger's homes, and maybe even on a moonshine operation. Lieutenant Lautzenhiser did a good job teaching me these things. We had firearms instructors come in and teach us how to use the gun we would be carrying. This was going to be a snub-nose .38 caliber revolver with a two-inch barrel.

You had to be good to use that gun and hit a target at fifty yards while at the firing range. I had fired my father's gun that was just like the one they gave me, but I had only shot at some bowling pins in a quarry. When I shot at those pins, I had no clue where my bullet went when I shot at it and missed. Now I was being trained for real. I was taught well on how to handle that gun. It took a few months to get it down, but I did.

After a four-week recruit school, we all graduated, and the new officers were given their assignments. I had already been assured I was going to be assigned to the Madison District, which I was. Another recruit, Phil McBride, was also being sent there. Phil had been working as a police officer with the Indiana University Police Department and was making a change in jobs. He was going to return to IU to work for a couple of weeks before reporting to Madison. From what I understood, this was something about getting his state pension moved over to another department.

I was sworn in, issued the gun, some extra bullets, handcuffs, some law books, and keys to my state car. This was a car I would be using, which was only temporary until my unmarked car was issued to me. The car they were giving me was a huge Chevrolet, landy-acht-type car with big seals of the State of Indiana on each side. We only had limited police powers to enforce ABC laws, rules, and regulations. We didn't have lights, sirens, or even two-way radios.

I reported to the Madison District office the following Monday morning at 8:00 a.m. The districts each had a lieutenant in charge, a sergeant, and however many officers that were assigned. Madison had five officers, including me. We initially were covering a fifteen-county area and that later increased to over twenty counties. It had been made real clear to me while in recruit school that the department used reassignment as a form of punishment. Officers working up in the big cities, Indianapolis, Fort Wayne, Gary, and La Porte knew that if they screwed up, they'd be sent to Madison. Except for having to either have to move or live out of a motel all week, I couldn't and still don't understand how working in Southern Indiana was bad. I knew if I screwed up, they'd send me to the La Porte District. That was a four-hour drive from home. If you couldn't enforce the laws in your district, they moved you. It wouldn't be a problem for me, I didn't want to go anywhere.

When I arrived that morning, I met the sergeant. I soon learned that all the officers called him Sarge. He had been on the job since 1951. That was the year I was born! Sarge told me that most of the officers at the district including the lieutenant were on vacation, and he didn't know what to do with me until the lieutenant returned in a couple of weeks. A couple of weeks?

To make a long wary story short, I sat in that office for two weeks. I read old reports in the file cabinets, got real familiar with the inspection forms we used, and read some interesting reports. I actually found an old report with Elliot Ness's name in it. These reports were ancient.

After two weeks of complete boredom, Phil McBride arrived. He quickly learned that he, too, would be waiting until the lieutenant returned. I tried not to laugh when, after two days, Phil whispered to me, "Is this what you have been doing since you got here?" I shook my head yes and looked away. Things will get better, I told myself; they had to.

Then after a couple of more days, it was about 3:00 p.m. on Friday afternoon, Sarge abruptly called out, "Jack, Phil, step up here [to his desk]!" This was a small office. I actually didn't have any problem hearing what he said while at my desk. Sarge had a hearing problem that stemmed from an old war injury, and we all always understood that.

Sarge told us we were being sent to North Vernon to conduct an undercover investigation regarding a complaint of gambling at a bar called the Nip 'n' Sip. Sarge told us to take our ties off and go in there, drink a beer or two, and report back our observations. He specifically mentioned we were to not take any sort of action.

Phil had a land yacht just like mine, and we both didn't hesitate to get into our cars and drive toward North Vernon. The town is about fifteen minutes north on State Road 7. Phil followed me up the highway and about a quarter of a mile away from Madison, I pulled off the road so I could speak with Phil. He and I just had to vent! We didn't feel free to talk much back at the office, so we had a lot of frustrations to talk about. We thought this assignment was quite unusual since we'd been cooped up so long, but we agreed to drive to North Vernon, find this bar, and then find a place to hide these huge state-sealed rides. We did just that. We found the Nip 'n' Sip and parked a block away. And we took off our ties. We walked to the bar, and upon entering the quaint tavern, we saw the bartender, a man about sixty years of age, and a couple of customers sitting at the bar drinking their beer. These guys looked like old farmers. Phil and I looked about as conspicuous as those ABC guys back in Louisville a couple of years earlier. The beer tasted great. It was so cold! Dead silence was the name of any game at the bar. I felt very paranoid about these people at the bar knowing who we were. I never thought why I would have such a feeling, wanting to do a good job and all. The closest thing I saw concerning gambling was a set of dice in a shot glass next to the cash register. Phil and I both drank two beers and left. We walked away, and while outside, I mentioned how weird that was in that place and suggested we find another place to have a beer and talk.

We found a place about a block away that was just opening for business. The woman owner and a lady friend were the only ones inside. We ordered a couple of beers, and after the owner brought them, she went toward the front of the bar and sat in a booth with her friend. Phil went to the restroom, and I started that feeling all over again that these women even knew who we were! I went over to the jukebox and dropped some money in it and selected some songs. Not that I was in the mood, but I wanted to have a conversation and not be overheard. The first song that played has stuck with me all these years. I guess it shows to some degree how this excise police experience was affecting me. Anytime now when I hear Jim Croce sing "Operator," I have to stop for a moment and reflect.

Phil and I finished our beers, we both expressed our frustrations, and agreed things would get better when the lieutenant returned. That was supposed to be Monday. We returned to our cars and he headed home to Orleans and I drove to Jeffersonville.

Things did get quite a bit better. The other officers returned to work from their vacations, and we went "out in the field" with them until we could be set out on our own.

Just a couple of months into the job, I received a telephone call from Chief Parker at the Jeffersonville Police Department. The chief told me had an opening, and that I could have it if I wanted it. I told him no. Knowing that the real job I wanted more than anything in the world was to work there, I had turned it down. I told Chief Parker that the excise police had just hired me (which he knew), sent me to recruit school, and I wasn't a *quitter*. He seemed to understand. I have thought back to that call many times and realized I was a person of principle and wasn't one to use a police appointment just as a "stepping stone," and that is why I turned him down. Looking back, I wish I'd quit the excise police the following day and accepted the job. Such a phone call from the chief should have been treasured and not taken as lightly as I did seem to have taken it. I was still learning. I really didn't have anyone to lean on, ask for advice, or learn from. I felt I was going through my life as a student of living.

The excise police job was good though. Monday through Thursdays, we basically did administrative work. That included annual inspections of permit premises, inspections for license renewals, inspected applicants for alcoholic beverage permits, and an Excise Officer attended the monthly meetings of the local ABC boards in each county. All of this kept us busy. You drove a couple of hundred miles each day.

Your workday didn't start until you arrived at the office. We were never allowed to log any overtime, ever. One of the best pieces of advice I received from other officers was to keep a personal diary of everything you did. This included car mileage, counties you went to, why you went there, case report numbers, and so on.

Friday and Saturday, work was in the evenings. We would work together and travel to wherever the sergeant or lieutenant sent us. You were always given a work assignment sheet each and every day telling you what to do.

These weekend, evenings usually involved arresting underage people buying alcohol, taking them to a justice of the peace, and citing the permit premises with any violations. If you worked on Sunday, that usually involved making buys from bootleggers. These were people who sold beer and whiskey from their cars or homes on Sunday. These bootleggers surely knew their customers, but I never had much of a problem making buys. Being a young man in his twenties and trying to appear you need a drink got to be a skill. After all, you didn't want to work all Saturday night, get a few hours' sleep, and then drive fifty or a hundred miles to some little town in some remote area to make a buy and fail. Get it and get done and get home was the rule. If you did make a buy, you prepared a search warrant for the bootlegger's home or place of *business*, and other officers would take a few state troopers with them the following Sunday and raid the guy.

My very first arrest in my life was while I was working one Friday evening with Rieke Meyer. He assured me I would be making an arrest soon. This was around 7:00 p.m., and we were at a fast-food hamburger place in New Albany. Meyer parked the car in the lot and told me to just wait. A few minutes went by, and some teenagers arrived. They went inside the restaurant and came out a few minutes later carrying their sacks of food. Meyer told me, "They have beer." What? I never saw any beer. He explained that I should watch them. They were sitting in their car eating, and they didn't carry any drinks out when they came outside. He was right. We went over and checked. They had a cooler of beer iced down in the rear seat. They were all underage. I think we arrested three of them and took them to the justice of the peace at Floyds Knobs. Well, I did make my first arrests. I thought about that night many times. I had set my goals much higher than this. I wanted to catch bank robbers and killers. I was catching kids with six-packs.

I checked many bars, VFWs, American Legions, package stores, grocery stores, and the few nightclubs in my district many times over the four years I worked for the excise police. I felt bad when I had to tell the man in New Albany he couldn't serve cans of beer from a cooler at the front counter of his new fast-food restaurant. He'd have to move the beer. I really felt bad when I was sent to a small town to perform a final inspection for a liquor store's new location. The owner had bought this building, renovated it, submitted his plans to the ABC, and when I got there, I nixed it all. He was too close to a school. I remeasured that building every way I could, but it couldn't be approved. Someone should have caught that a long time earlier, but I wasn't part of that process.

Back in the 1970s, a bar couldn't have dancing without a permit. We had to conduct inspections to ensure the dance area was the right size, in the right location, and whatever that was used as a border couldn't allow a drink to be set on it.

Sitting on a local county board was something I did periodically. Basically, the excise police office received applications that would be considered by a local board and whatever officer was assigned merely carried those applications to the meeting and handed to the board to consider. This was the only time an officer's political affiliation played a part in the performance of their duties.

You see, the three-member board consisted of a member appointed by that county's commissioners, county council, and the mayor of that county's largest city. It was set up so there were two members from one party and a member from the other party. The excise officer that was sent to partake in the meeting had to be a member of whatever affiliation it would take to have two Democrats and two Republicans. The excise officer normally just delivered the applications and sat on the board and observed questioning of the applicant. The excise officer offered answers to legal and administrative questions.

There was this one time I sat on the local board at Washington County. I hadn't even looked at the applications I was bringing to that morning meeting to the circuit courtroom when I walked into a packed room. This wasn't totally unusual for this county. I had walked into packed meetings before when remonstrators were protesting liquor licenses and dance permits. This time was eventful.

There was a package liquor store that had its license tied up for quite a while in some sort of legal matter in a federal court. On this day, it was apparent the matter had been resolved, and the license was ordered available for applicants to vie for. The people who had been running it had evidently went straight to the ABC office in Indianapolis the day the license was ordered *available*, and I had brought that application with me. I also had brought an application from a local businessman for the same license. The president of the local board asked me who we were going to hear first, and I could feel the tension in the air when he asked me that question. I threw it back at him and told him he was president of the local board, and he was to make that decision. He and the other three members all agreed I should be the one to decide. I was a bit disappointed with these three members. They had been appointed to make decisions, and they couldn't make this one easy decision. This was beginning to become a lesson in my life.

Here I sat in this crowded courtroom, a stranger to most but known to represent the state of Indiana at that moment. You could hear a pin drop when I was told that this decision was mine to make. My mind was racing for an answer. I hadn't been trained what to do in such a situation, so I just let my common sense decide. The applications had time stamps on them. When the ABC received the application, apparently they stuck it in a time clock-type device because that's what the time stamp looked like. I told the board that Mr. So and So's application should be heard first since it was time-stamped several days before the local businessman.

The local board went through the normal questioning process of this man and afterward unanimously voted to grant him the license. After that vote, I suggested to the board that the second applicant should then be considered. They argued with me, stating why waste the time, the first applicant had been granted the license. I tried to explain to the board that the local board's vote results were actually a recommendation to the state ABC whether or not to grant a license to an applicant. But one of the members stood up, here in front of everyone in this crowded courtroom, and announced that he had firsthand information that I was part owner of the liquor store, and he then stormed out of the meeting and went to a restroom. Someone went to the restroom to try to get him to return to the meeting, but I was told he had quit the local board and would not be returning. I learned something about myself at that moment. I never said a word and kept the meeting going. I never discussed any of the matter with anyone there that day. I was impressed with myself. Standing up in front of that crowd and saying anything would have been unprofessional.

The original owner of the store did get his license back. I guess everyone thought I was getting a cut. The store always did good business. I thought many times if I were a crook, I'd made a little money on that one.

I never heard anything from the ABC about how I performed that day. Other than relating the events to the officers back at the office, I never heard a word. But the ABC immediately quit time-stamping applications.

There was a certain county that had a local board member whose business was selling cleaning supplies. On more than one occasion, the excise police office received calls from owners of new businesses who had just appeared at this county's local board meeting and had their alcoholic beverage permit application approved, that upon return to their new business to find a quantity of cleaning supplies delivered and waiting, along with an invoice.

We never had time to initiate many investigations on places selling to minors. When we were assigned to investigate a place, I always knew that whenever it got to the point that someone called the excise police, it must be bad. Whether it was the local police or citizen complaining, whenever we responded, it sure didn't take long to catch a kid buying something.

One evening, we were checking a liquor store on a complaint, and while we were filling out arrest slips in the parking lot on a couple of kids we just caught, more minors showed up and went in and bought beer. We arrested seven or eight minors that evening, including a daughter of the mayor of the largest city in that county. When I attended that county's local board meeting the following week, that mayor's appointee to the board stood up and made a loud accusation that I owned a competing liquor store down the road from the one where the arrests were made. This time, it ran through my mind to tell this joker to sit down and shut the heck up, but I sat there and looked at him. My nonresponse to his remark obviously caused him embarrassment. He sat down and never said a word about it again. I actually waited for him to storm out of the room and quit like the last guy. But he didn't. That guy was always amicable when I attended the meetings in the past, and I was surprised to see this side of him come out. But I was learning quickly about the politics of the job.

One thing I have learned about myself is that I have been smart enough to make every experience a learning experience. I knew that back in the days when I worked as a hospital orderly and witnessed autopsies, badly injured people, and surgery that I planned on taking those experiences to my future career as a police officer. I knew I'd see those things then, and I would be somewhat prepared. I was learning that I had a whole lot more to learn about a lot of things.

Probably one of the biggest eye-openers I had began one Monday morning when I reported to work at the Madison office. Sarge gave Phil McBride and me a worksheet, sending us to Bartholomew County to perform quite a few renewal inspections. We used this Form 37 that the excise police had to fill out for these inspections. There were an unusual number of inspections we needed to do, so Phil and I quickly got a plan together to go there and knock them out systematically. This county is where Columbus is the county seat. I always enjoyed going there to work. There were plenty of places to find lunch, and the Columbus Police and Bartholomew County Sheriff's office was a place where we were always welcome, and I enjoyed visiting when we could. These officers were working in bigger departments, very professional, and I could learn from them.

We went there that morning, and we did do everything on the worksheet. You never *didn't* do something you were assigned to do. You just got it done. One of the places we were sent to inspect for renewal was this country club. Phil said it was way out and would be best for him and I to check it last as it was somewhat out of town. I had never heard of the place, but Phil told me he'd been there once before.

It was probably three o'clock in the afternoon when we arrived at this country club. It was way out in the country, and when you arrive, you see there was a golf course, nice clubhouse, pool, and a lot of greenery. It was a nice place.

When we pulled into the parking lot, we had to find a place to park. The lot was fairly full of cars. More than anything, I was glad we were at our last stop. We still had to drive back to Madison when we finished, do all of our paperwork, and drive home. That was an hour drive just to go home. I was getting tired by this stop.

We walked up to the clubhouse and tried to enter. The door was locked. This really surprised me. There was a lot full of cars, people out playing golf, and the door was locked. But Phil told me that the last time he was there, the door was locked then too, and there was a door back by the pool. I followed Phil to the rear of the building, and I saw a sliding glass door, and the curtains inside were pulled closed. I slid the door open and parted the curtains and saw immediately I was looking into a darkened barroom. It was very obvious the bar was closed as there wasn't anyone in sight, and the lights were off. I couldn't figure it out. I hollered "hello" into the building while still standing outside the door, and I could see a hallway adjacent to the barroom had a light on, and I saw a young woman enter the hall apparently responding to my call. This young woman told me the bar was closed. I told her we were with the Indiana State Excise Police, and I showed her my credentials as I entered the darkened bar area. She told me again the bar was closed, and I explained to her that the alcoholic beverage license was due for renewal, and we were there to perform the required inspection for that process. The woman told me she was a secretary, and we should return later. I told her the inspection would only take a few minutes and a delay may possibly cause the permit to be suspended pending renewal. She agreed and told us to go ahead and do what we needed to do. Phil and I quickly resumed the routine that we had followed all day long. I examined the alcoholic beverage permit on the wall, posted as required, and filled out the inspection form. Phil disappeared from my sight going to other areas of the club. According to law, and conditions of the permit, all of the club was considered permit premises and excise police had the same as search warrant privileges to enter any part.

The young woman obviously appeared very uncomfortable with our presence. She stood with her arms crossed, and I saw her shoulders seemed rigid. This was a body language that told me she felt uncomfortable because she was alone in the building with a couple of men she didn't know. I talked to her about the renewal process to make some attempt to reassure her we were on official business and maybe she would be more comfortable with me talking to her. Phil was out of her sight as well while I spoke with her and did my paperwork. It was just after a few minutes, Phil returned and came up to me and whispered in my ear. Whatever Phil had to say at that moment, I felt was undermining every effort I was making to get this young woman to try to relax.

Phil whispered to me that I needed to see what he had found in another room. There was nothing I could say to this secretary. I felt she was very intimidated now, not only by our being there but also by our whispering. I asked her to excuse me while I checked something. Phil led me to this room where I saw several large, partially opened crates, containing gambling equipment. There were tables and at least one roulette wheel that I saw. These devices were made with some outstanding wood and craftsmanship. I had never been to a casino, but these items certainly were made for the best. Having now been to many casinos many years later, I still know those things were top of the line. It was top-shelf.

Phil looked at me to make a decision as to what action to take. I had done this thing before. He and I had been to a club in New Albany and, when we found slot machines, called the local police.

I recalled the controversy that event caused, and I kept in mind we were at an exclusive country club in one of the richest counties in the country. Plus, at the New Albany club, he and I played the machines for a while before being confronted by club managers.

I told Phil that we would file a report and leave. I knew that wasn't what he wanted to hear, but that's the decision I made. I did have that two weeks on him sitting in the office back then and that did give me a little seniority. It was a very good decision in retrospect.

We did finish our inspection quickly after that and left. We returned to Madison and filed our paperwork.

The following day, I had been assigned post duty. That meant I sat at the Sarge's desk and answered the phone all day. Hardly anyone ever came to the office except the officers. But if someone, such as a permit holder came by, it would be the person working post duty to deal with them.

Sarge was off that day, and Lieutenant Watson was out somewhere "in the field."

It was around two o'clock in the afternoon when I answered the phone, and it was Major Portolese calling. The major asked me if Lieutenant Watson was in, and I told him he was out but was expected to return pretty soon. Major Portolese asked me who had went to that particular country club the day before, and I told him Phil and I had went there for a renewal inspection. Major Portolese immediately told me we had broken into the clubhouse, and they were making a complaint.

I don't remember what else he said, but I did tell him he had not hired a *burglar*. It was at that very moment Lieutenant Watson walked into the office with another officer. I know he saw a look on my face showing concern, anger, or something. All I did was say to Major Portolese at that moment was, "Hold on, Lieutenant Watson just walked in," and I held an outstretched hand with the phone to Lieutenant Watson.

Lieutenant Watson asked me who was on the phone, and I told him. He said he'd take the call in his office. Once Lieutenant Watson picked up his extension, I hung my phone up. I had so many confused thoughts going through my mind during the few moments

Lieutenant Watson spoke with the major. The office wasn't that big, and you could pretty well hear what was said anywhere in the building. It wasn't but a minute or two after he was heard hanging his phone up when he reentered the office where I was and told the officer he had just walked in with to come with him and that they were going to Columbus for a meeting with the Indiana State Police and the county prosecutor. Before he left, he asked what had happened at the club, and I told him. I especially mentioned the part about the rear sliding door since they thought I had *burglarized* the place. I also told him all about the gambling equipment there. Lieutenant Watson just shook his head in disbelief that he was going to have to deal with this issue, and he and the other officer left the building. I felt he knew where this thing was coming from.

The next couple of hours were probably the worst hours in my police career at that point. I closed the office at 5:00 p.m. and drove home. I was off the next two days, Wednesday and Thursday, as scheduled. I could not believe what I was having to deal with, and I truly was concerned. I knew we hadn't done anything wrong, but I knew how things happen to police officers. I felt I had an issue I was going to have to deal with that wasn't going to be much fun. I hadn't committed a crime. What was going on?

I was trying to be a career police officer and knew I may or may not have made the right decision to join the excise police, but I had so much fortitude built up inside me I was going to stand my ground and stand tall. I hadn't done anything wrong. Those two days off were very long. While I was off those two days, I did run into an attorney friend of mine. He knew the Alcoholic Beverage Commission quite well. He was well established in Clark County as the *go-to guy* to get things done when it came to permit applications, renewal issues, or whatever. I told him about the accusations, and he told me that if anything came of it, to call him.

Well, I returned to work the following Friday evening. Since it was a Friday, that meant we worked evenings and probably were going to check complaints of minors. Rieke Meyer had arranged to pick me up. He lived in Clarksville, and whenever we could double up on weekends, we did. I rode with him to the Madison office, arriving just before 5:00 p.m. That's when the office closed, and we tried to arrive before the sergeant or lieutenant left for the day. Otherwise, we knew that upon arrival, we could find an assignment sheet telling us what to do that evening as well as for Saturday and Sunday.

Sarge was still sitting at his desk when we arrived. Looking back, he probably was awaiting my arrival. When Meyer and I entered the office, Sarge was at his desk. Meyer picked up the assignment sheet for that evening at that desk, and it wasn't a split second before Sarge asked me, "Fleeman, what the hell happened with you and McBride at Bartholomew County Monday?" I knew what he was asking. I had been asking myself the question all week. I replied, "Sarge, we went there for a Form 37 investigation, and when I was working post duty Tuesday, Major Portolese called me and said we had burglarized the country club." I told Sarge that I had told Major Portolese that he hadn't hired a burglar. I truly trusted Major Portolese, and when I had told him that remark, I was concerned that he took offense. I have always thought about why I felt that way. Major Portolese must have really sensed a problem with me.

Sarge didn't wait a second to tell me, "They are filing charges against you." It was at that moment that I learned another thing about Jack Fleeman. I reached over, picked up Sarge's telephone, and began to make a call. He quickly asked, "Who are you calling?" And I replied, "My attorney." He ordered me to hang the phone up which I did. I was sorta glad because I didn't have a clue of what number to dial, but I was fed up at this point and ready to take a stand. Sarge told me to calm down and not to worry. He did say that when Lieutenant Watson went to that country club, the county prosecutor was there, the Indiana State Police, as well as club officials. Sarge told me I would need to speak with Lieutenant Watson about what was happening.

I wouldn't see Lieutenant Watson until the next week. It really upset me that nobody seemed to want to keep me informed, and it was obvious that Sarge was messing with me.

I was in the office for about fifteen minutes while Meyer and I prepared to leave for our workday. But before he left, Sarge commented to me that I should have known better than to ever gone to that country club in the first place. I asked what he meant, remembering he had sent McBride and me there, and he stated that traditionally country clubs are closed in Indiana on Monday.

I thought, *Well, whoop-de-do!* Here he sends me there and tells me I should have known better than going. I told him that I wasn't now nor ever a member of any club like that, and I didn't know about this *rule*.

I just wanted to be a police officer, and if I had said any smart remark back to him, they'd fire me in an instant. After all, as far as I knew, I was headed to jail, and the major had accused me of burglarizing that place. I knew the truth at every step of the way. I had witnessed so much political corruptness, and I knew to keep my mouth shut. My thoughts were now toward finding a way out of this job and keeping a good record.

I hung in there, and the following week, I met with Lieutenant Watson. I told him what Sarge had told me, and he responded that he didn't know why I had been told that because the matter was closed.

Lieutenant Watson told me that after he left me that previous Tuesday, he went to the country club and, upon arrival, met all the top law enforcement officials of the county there as well as the top officials of the country club. He told me he was advised by someone of the nature of the concern that two excise officers had broken into the clubhouse through the sliding glass door at the barroom. Knowing what I had told him, and probably well experienced at this stuff, Lieutenant Watson spoke with the club manager and asked him to show him (Watson) the door through which they entered. He told me all the representatives there went to the barroom and were shown which door was supposedly forced open. He told me he asked the club manager to allow him to step outside the door and then to lock the door. He said that before he exited the doorway, the manager commented, "We have had problems with this door." Lieutenant Watson stated he went outside the door, was locked out, and then without any problem, easily slid the door open.

Lieutenant Watson stated that after some conversation, it was agreed that the excise officers made an *honest mistake*, and the matter was closed. Lieutenant Watson stated he did counter that point by mentioning that his officers reported finding gambling equipment in newly opened crates in another room. He stated that all the officials toured the building and no such items were found, or known about by the club officials. Go figure.

You know, after hearing Lieutenant Watson tell me the story, I fully understood what had happened to me. This was part of law enforcement. I was really getting the whole picture now. But I was still bothered by the fact he hadn't called me that evening and explained his findings and let me feel relief. I was already figuring out why Sarge messed with me.

Politics Sticking its Nose
into Police Work

I never heard another thing about that incident, and I was never sent back to that country club.

I was coming to realize that politics was more than voting for an electoral candidate. I didn't think I would have to deal with politics in this manner.

I gave the event plenty of thought. I eventually began to realize that this was something I would have to deal with in this job, and Lieutenant Watson probably didn't even think to call me about it. He had told me so many stories of his own, even one of being shot in the back while walking to his apartment after work while assigned to another district, that I felt I was being a *small thinker* about how things are, and I was just beginning to learn how things went.

I was starting to get my guard up now. But I wasn't sure how far I'd have to have it up.

The job had some low points like that, but for the most part, I had a blast. I was involved in investigations, seeming to make a difference, and even though I was involved in a limited area of law enforcement, I felt good. But I still wanted to do *real* police work. You know, catch the robbers and killers.

There was this one Saturday night when I was working with two other officers. We had been assigned to work Brown County, which was all the way to the far northwest corner of our district, and also follow up on complaints straight south to Harrison County, which was at the southwest corner of our district. We had a lot of miles to cover and a lot of things to do, but this assignment would keep us out probably until 5:00 a.m. or 6:00 a.m., and we wouldn't have to come back out on Sunday to work on bootleggers.

We ended up at the Harrison County jail at Corydon booking a prisoner sometime after 2:00 a.m., and we knew we were making good time, considering what all we had to get done that night. While at the jail, the dispatcher told us that the Indiana State Police had heard we were at the jail and asked if we would assist them at Elizabeth. This is a small town, close to the Ohio River, at the south portion of Harrison County. The state police had a squad of troopers that had patrolled throughout their district that night and wanted us to help them when they arrived at Elizabeth. That small town was remote and did have a couple of bars, and the main problem they usually had were teenagers drinking and partying in the street in the wee hours.

We did help the state police and ended up finding things pretty calm in town. But the three of us excise guys found a guy passed out in the seat of his pickup truck in front of the post office. We woke him up and locked him up for public intoxication.

Probably a month later, the three of us got subpoenaed for a trial on this guy at the Harrison Circuit Court. We all appeared, and they did have a trial rule for separation of witnesses, meaning we had to stay out in the hallway, and we didn't hear each other's testimony.

This guy, who we had arrested, had hired this attorney from New Albany named Mike McDaniel. We knew McDaniel's reputation. He was good and got a lot of crooks *off*. Most police in the area didn't like him because of that. He was considered the *enemy*.

Well, we all testified, and we couldn't figure out what the questions was about this guy's guilt. He was passed out drunk when we found him.

After a while, we were told the trial was over, and we all could enter the courtroom to hear what the judge had to say.

There weren't too many people in the courtroom, and the judge seemed ready to address us excise officers more than anything else.

I have always remembered what the judge said that morning about his findings. I have related this to many young police officers whenever I had the chance, and after a couple of decades, I have joked about it with Mr. McDaniel always remarking about what a lesson I learned on that case. (Mike says he doesn't remember the trial. Years later, I came to realize why the area police didn't like him. He was smart enough to look for weaknesses in their cases, and he did his job.)

The judge stated that morning, when he handed down his ruling, that all three of us (excise officers) came into the court and testified about how we had found the defendant. The judge stated we all testified using the jargon that they taught us at *police school*. He said we all told the court about this guy having the odor of alcoholic beverages about his person, his clothing was in disarray, he was unsteady on his feet, and he spoke with slurred speech, etc.

The judge stated that when we were asked about which one of us was driving the car we were in, we all gave different answers. He said the man was therefore found *not guilty*, and he cut him loose.

I have had so much enjoyment with that free lesson in police work and preparing for trial. When we left the courtroom, the three of us argued all the way out to the street who was driving when we locked that guy up, and we all three did have different recollections! Heck, we were so tired from all the miles and work we had done that night, and we had, like we usually did, taken turns driving!

I don't think we ever figured out who drove the car to Elizabeth. And I know it wasn't me, like one officer testified!

The judge was right, and I fully have understood about how he came to that decision. Here, you have a local resident sleeping in his car and some out-of-town-state guys come in and accuse him of a crime. He was asleep when we found him. This guy had to hire an expensive (and respected) lawyer to defend himself, and these people, that the state had *sent in* to that small town, cannot even say who was driving their car. It was a very good lesson for me. That is what I have come to understand as good local justice. The judge was right about everything and wanted to be sure his county's residents were treated fairly. If that drunk had been some out-of-towner who found his drunk butt in Elizabeth that night by some mistake, the judge would have been right to have perhaps made a different decision. I have always hoped that the young police officers I have told this story to over the years have understood what I was telling them when I told them this story.

There was this one city court judge who taught me another lesson on one of his official acts.

I had made a bootleg buy off of this guy in a small town one Sunday. I think I bought a case of beer off of him. I was proud of getting that buy because other officers had failed in the past. You see, it's not the fact he is unlicensed, inasmuch as he hurts the local businesses that sell beer the rest of the week. The people could have purchased their beer Saturday from them.

One day during the following week, I prepared a search warrant to be served on this bootlegger the following Sunday. Sunday morning is the best time to serve the warrant because the bootlegger will be "loaded up" with his booze and this usually helps your court case.

Well, I took the search warrant to the city court in that same county and asked the clerk if the judge could take a look at it. The clerk sent me straight into open court when everybody and their brothers were, as well as a school class, on a field trip. The judge was told by the clerk the purpose of my visit, and he called me up to the bench. I appreciated his desire to serve me quickly, but to my surprise, he verbally told the students (as well as everyone else in the courtroom) the purpose of my visit, what I wanted, and he proceeded to read my affidavit of probable cause out loud. I stood in front of the judge and knew there was nothing I could do except to hope that nobody *spilled the beans* and word got back to the bootlegger. Well, it did. The officers who went there that next Sunday didn't find him nor any beer when they searched his house.

The judge was fairly new and was trying to do the right thing. He and I later became good friends, and I sometimes enjoyed reminding him of that day in his court.

I was sent to this one small town occasionally to try to make a *buy* off of this old guy who sold half-pints of whiskey from his car. I watched him meet several customers, and whenever his business was *brisk*, I would walk toward him. He always suspected me and usually drove away. One Sunday, he aimed his car at me and *floored it.* I jumped up on the sidewalk and decided then that I was finished with this one. I returned to my office the following day and told my lieutenant that someone else needed to work on this guy.

One Sunday, my lieutenant and I were driving around this small town just checking things to see if we could spot bootlegging. We knew what to look for.

While driving down this small street that had ditches on each side of it and little ramshackle houses on each side, the lieutenant pointed out where an old-time bootlegger lived that had been busted a few times before I was hired.

Just as we drove past this guy's house, I saw him step outside. We were driving my unmarked police-car-looking excise car and knew we couldn't do anything like attempt a buy while driving it, so I suggested to the lieutenant that we go back to the old guy's house and maybe he'd tell us where we could buy something. We knew he'd know who we were by our car, and the fact that the lieutenant had arrested him a couple times before.

We went around the block and pulled into the driveway at this guy's house and spoke out to him and asked, "How you doin' today?" He walked up to our car as I spoke, and he replied, "Things were slow." We asked him where someone could get something to drink, and we figured he send us somewhere across town. But he asked us what we wanted, and I immediately thought, *He doesn't know who we are.* I told him we were looking for "a couple of halves" (meaning two half-pints of whiskey), and he said, "Well, I know you aren't excise, they only ask for one just to make a buy." I replied, "No, we want two!" We ended up buying two halves from this guy. I don't think we ever came back there. We talked about returning and telling him who we were and maybe he'd tell on someone else, but we just let it go.

Bootlegging was plentiful in this small town, and he'd been busted more than anyone else.

If you worked in an area close to the Ohio River, someone could easily go to Kentucky on a Sunday and buy their beer. But whiskey was bootlegged everywhere on Sundays, and the further you were from Kentucky, the more beer you could buy. This *rule* didn't apply to events like turkey shoots. They sold draft beer as a service to the attendees. It didn't matter how close you were to Kentucky when it came to those events.

We received a complaint from the sheriff of this one county telling us that this guy was planning some sort of big picnic the following Sunday afternoon and was advertising that beer was being served. The picnic was being held at a municipal park, and a big crowd was expected.

I was off work that Sunday when three officers were sent to investigate. When I returned to work the next day, I asked them what had happened when they went to that big picnic. The officers who had went there were all in the office, and when I asked that question, they all laughed. They told me that as they drove down this long unpaved driveway into the park, they came across a sign advertising this picnic. It was on the sign they learned it was picnic being held on behalf of a candidate running in the next election against the sheriff who had called us. They chuckled as they told me they couldn't get away from that function fast enough. They told me how the lane they were driving on was long, without a place to turn around, and they drove all the way into the park and up to where the picnic was being held. They said there was a huge crowd like the sheriff had reported. The officers joked that the huge crowd is what he was really worried about and hoped the excise police would put a damper on the festivities. That didn't happen.

We tried to always detect when we might be being *used* for someone's political gain. The excise police had had a long history of being a political tool and with the new *attitude* of trying to professionalize the outfit being a goal of the administration, we younger officers did what we could do to try to help our image. We wanted to be police officers.

One time, Phil McBride and I had been scheduled to work in one county answering complaints on Saturday evening, and we were scheduled to assist Jeffersonville Police, at their request, on bootleggers there on Sunday.

Phil had called me and told me he had been told about this huge party in Decatur County at a social hall at a small town named Millhousen. The party was being held for this guy going into the military and fliers being circulated made it clear beer was going to be available with an admission price. We always were made aware of an event that the ABC had sanctioned and issued a temporary permit, and we knew this party was not on that list.

I told Phil to call the lieutenant and advise him of what he had learned, and we'd do whatever he told us to do. Phil called me back soon and said the lieutenant told him that he and I should first go to the Indiana State Police post at Seymour and advise the commander there of the complaint, and unless they were planning on checking this party out, we should go check the party out, and if help was needed, ask the state police if they could be called.

I met Phil at the post at Seymour, and we found Sergeant Leffler in charge. He told us he hadn't heard anything about this planned party and explained he was one of the sergeants over that district. He also told us he would be in Decatur County later in the evening because all of the troopers in the county would be attending the local FOP dance at Greensburg, which was the county seat.

Sergeant Leffler told us he'd be at the Greensburg City Police Department, and we could report there to give a report. Phil and I left and headed to Millhousen. I didn't remember having ever been there before. But this social hall, St. John's Hall, where the party was going to be, was a former church building.

Phil and I arrived at St. John's Hall before it was dark. The young people were arriving in droves. There were probably fifty minors there when we arrived, all entering the hall through a down-stairs doorway at the rear of the building.

It concerned me that I had been working in the county just two weeks earlier and had made several arrests of underage drinkers then. I didn't want *to be made* as cops so early in the evening. It worried me how we looked also. I wore my hair a little over my ears, but Phil, having been used to being a uniformed officer, wore white walls over his ears. That means he had his haircut clean and neat, just like a cop. Phil was also wearing those ultrashiny shoes uniformed police wore, even though we were plainclothes. *Well, oh well*, I thought, we were in this and had to check things out.

Phil and I were in my unmarked car and parked in a grassy area just outside St. John's Hall. We went in along with all the others who were arriving, and we had to pay a cover charge to go inside. We also got our hands stamped. As soon as I got my hand stamped, some guy slapped a half-empty bottle of vodka in my hand and said something about me having a good time. We saw kegs of beer being set up, and the odor of marihuana being smoked was obvious. We didn't stay long at all, maybe five minutes or less. We knew what we had. We returned to our car and drove toward Greensburg, which was about eight miles away. Traffic headed toward Millhousen coming from Greensburg was now bumper-to-bumper. One car had even went into a ditch along the road.

It was dark now when we arrived at Greensburg PD to meet Sergeant Leffler. He was there, and the police were telling us they were getting phone calls now about the traffic and this planned party. Sergeant Leffler knew we would need to do something. He was going to need to do something he hated to do—call over to the FOP Dance, which we could see was going on across the city's square where we were located. There we were, all of these cars, including several state police cars, parked outside at the dance, and we could hear the music. I remember so well of how I thought things would be different if Phil and I had attended that dance and didn't have to work that evening.

To make a long story short, Sergeant Leffler made that call to the dance, and within a few minutes, we saw those state police cars pulling away from the dance.

Sergeant Leffler made several phone calls and told us that a raiding party was being assembled, and everyone was going to meet at the state police post at Versailles in Ripley County. Phil and I drove there. Troopers from three state police districts were being called in for the raid.

I had suggested that some state undercover officers be sent inside prior to the raid since we knew drugs were there, but all of the undercover detectives were on a detail in another part of Indiana.

After everyone arrived at the Versailles Post, Sergeant Leffler briefed everybody and made assignments. I guess about twenty troopers were there to make the raid. Three troopers that normally worked in that area volunteered to go home and change into plainclothes. When they returned to the post, in order to ride with Phil and me to the party, I thought that they still looked like police. I told them that, and they reassured me they could deal with it. It just didn't seem like a party where you could wear a fishing hat and fit in.

Phil, these three troopers, and I were sent in to St. John's Hall first. We were told that after we entered the party, the rest of the troopers would arrive about five minutes later to raid the place. We needed to get inside first, and when the raid began, we needed to grab the money box at the front door. We needed it as evidence to demonstrate that this is a function opened to the public and not a private gathering.

When I pulled into another grassy area at the hall, we saw a lot more cars than we expected, and the troopers in the car quickly saw young people leaving cars to enter the party who would know them. The troopers decided to lie down in the back seat of my car, out of sight, until the raid went down. It made sense.

Phil and I went back inside the hall, and this time, things were a lot more crowded. I saw someone throw what appeared to be about a quarter pound of marihuana into a gas furnace. A band was playing, people were dancing, and draft beer was being handed out to anyone who wanted it. The basement room of the hall where this was happening had a low ceiling, and the loud music made conversation almost impossible.

It seemed a whole lot longer than five minutes while we're there, and I really began to worry someone would recognize us. It actually was approaching fifteen minutes since we had entered, and it was then I saw a guy I had arrested in Greensburg two weeks earlier. I immediately tried to yell loud enough for Phil to hear me that we needed to hide in the crowd. The music was so loud that he never did understand what I was trying to tell him. It wasn't a moment that passed before I realized Phil and I were surrounded by seven or eight guys along with the guy I had arrested. That guy tried to say something to me, but I couldn't hear what he said. I could use my imagination though, to know that Phil and I were in a jam. I pushed

Phil a little to make him aware of what was happening to us, and I reached for my concealed snub-nosed revolver and a can of mace I had hidden in my waistband. I wasn't quite sure what I was going to do with either weapon, but I knew one thing, I was going to be going home that evening all in one piece and not get hurt over this party. It was at the very moment I grabbed for the gun and mace that I immediately saw police nightsticks swinging at the entrance to the party. I left the gun and mace where I had them, and the raid was on!

I knew I was too far from the cashbox, and I hoped one of the other officers had grabbed it. But it disappeared.

The building was sealed, and nobody got away, except a few who were outside when the raid began. Windows were broken out from the inside by some of those inside. A few tried to escape, but they didn't, and the party was busted.

Eventually we all realized way too many people were going to be arrested, and plenty more than the Decatur County Jail, or any other county jail around could hold. We used school buses to haul everyone off to the National Guard Armory. Only the worst of those being arrested actually went to jail. In all, 184 people were arrested at the hall.

We seized the kegs that still had beer in them, and we picked enough pills and bags of pot up off the floor inside the hall that we filled up a couple of big soft drink cups.

Phil and I finished up doing some of the paperwork probably close to 4:00 a.m. Sergeant Leffler and another trooper told us to go ahead and leave and that they would finish up. Sergeant Leffler knew we had to head to Jeffersonville to help the city police there make more raids. This was going to be a very busy weekend for me.

We were about a two-hour drive away from Jeffersonville. Phil and I headed back to the Seymour State Police Post where his car was parked and headed toward Jeff.

Oh yeah, I did find out the reason the troopers were delayed with their arrival at St. John's Hall. It was that after leaving that state police post and heading down a country road toward Millhousen, one of the troopers needed to *relieve* himself before getting to this place, and the *idea* caught on quickly. They all stopped along the way and *took a whiz*. I can understand that!

Phil and I arrived at Jeffersonville almost at 7:00 a.m. This was the time we had arranged to meet the city police detectives. Rieke Meyer worked that day and met us as well. Phil and I were still sort of *reeling* from the excitement from the raid, and we found it hard to get the officers we were hooking up with to join in on our excitement. They were tired from getting up so early on a Sunday and going to work.

Anyhow, we all met and ate breakfast at a restaurant and got straight to work. We knew who we were targeting, and we did it. This one guy, a white guy, lived in a dilapidated house on Eighth Street in Jeffersonville was supposedly buying stolen property and selling whiskey on Sunday. Meyer attempted a buy, and he found that nobody was home. Jeff PD didn't have any information we could use to obtain up a search warrant for the house, so we decided to deal with this guy at a later time.

Jeff PD had their focus on two bootleggers they felt sure could be busted. This one guy, an older black man who lived in a little shack in the north end of town, was known to always sell whiskey on Sundays. And there was a black man who lived next door to him who didn't just sell but also allowed customers to stay and drink.

I hadn't too much experience dealing with black bootleggers. The excise police had a whole squad of black officers who focused their efforts toward black establishments. Those guys always impressed me. They had lots of experience and usually worked the bigger cities where there was more work for them to do. One of those officers was Jerry Daniels. He had been one of the original "Ink Spots."

The excise police also didn't usually obtain information for search warrants based on informant's information. However, the city police did this routinely and convinced us this would be our best bet to bust these guys.

The informant was being paid for his effort by the city police and told us early on that the older guy we wanted to bust didn't like him, and he knew he couldn't make a buy off of him. The other guy, who let customers hang out there, would be easy, and that's what we did. The informant went in there, made a buy, and met us a few blocks up the street. The city police kept the bottle, and we all agreed to call this a JPD case, and the excise were just assisting.

I was selected to type the search warrant. I have always found that even in later years, when a search warrant needed to be prepared, I was the lucky guy who got picked. I guess I found it easy, and I knew what needed to be included in such a document.

By the time we got the warrant signed by a judge, it was evening and getting dark. I surprised myself how all this activity kept me awake and very alert. I'd been working for over twenty-four hours at this point. The only downtime I had enjoyed was the drive from Greensburg and breakfast.

We went to this house and knocked on the door. The guy we were after was alone in the house and opened the door. We entered and told him to have a seat on his couch while we secured the residence. He complied, and a uniformed officer began to read him the warrant. I started to enter the kitchen to get started searching for evidence when I heard a sound I had never heard before but recognized what it was. I had my back to the guy while entering the kitchen, and it was at that moment he pulled a gun on the officer reading him the warrant. There were at least four uniformed officers that I had heard pull their guns and aim straight at him and order him to drop his gun. The sound I had heard was the steel brushing fiercely against the officer's leather holsters. He did surrender the gun, and the search proceeded. The Jeff city officers seemed so calm.

We took the evidence we found, the gun, and the suspect to police headquarters. Jeffersonville Police finished the paperwork, and I finally went home. It had been a long day. After going home, I found it very difficult to think all about the events I had experienced since leaving for work the day before. Fatigue was playing in on me, and I took that as a lesson to remember how important it is to pace myself better in the future.

On the Lighter Side

I was enjoying this job so very much, but, deep down inside me, I knew I would someday be a Jeffersonville police officer. That is what I wanted.

Whenever I tell someone about my experiences with the excise police, I always tell about the Indy 500. The excise police officers were always assigned to work the Indianapolis 500 Time Trials at Speedway, Indiana.

I don't remember doing anything except being there, hanging out with other officers, and enjoying the event. One year, we did arrest one person who was passed out. At least I did assist on that arrest. There might have been a couple of more who got arrested, but I hadn't been involved if there were.

The most memorable event I experienced was the year the first two-way radio communications were being used between a driver and his crew. A. J. Foyt was the driver.

I had been issued a lapel pin that gave me full access to anywhere at the track and that included Gasoline Alley and the Pit.

When Foyt was preparing to qualify and his crew was setting up his antenna at the pit, I was there. I stood within a few feet of the whole thing. I had ran into an Indiana state trooper friend of mine, and he and I stood there and watched the event unfold. This trooper, Curtis Wells, had attended high school with me, and we both chuckled about being so close to the action. I did have a concern when it was about 5:00 p.m. and the ABC Wide World of Sports went live as I realized I was on live national TV and a whole lot of people were watching. I didn't think for even a moment that any of my loved ones at home might be watching since I knew none of them had any interest in car racing. I did think that my chief or another high-ranking officer at the excise police might be watching me and knew I was goofing off. I didn't go back and brag to the other officers of that experience because I didn't want to put them on the spot in case I did get into some *hot water*. I never heard a word about it. Darn it! That meant nobody I knew even recognized me.

I did, however, have some friends from back home who told me several days later that they were amused how much this guy in pit row looked just like me! I don't think he believed me at first when I told him it was me he had seen.

I worked the Time Trials from 1974 through 1977. It was a time when you got to leave your district and work with officers from other parts of the state whom you didn't see too often. We would be sent to the Indiana Law Enforcement Academy at Plainfield to be housed. The officers attending the academy had been sent home Friday afternoon with a group of state troopers and excise officers to move in for sleeping quarters by that evening. There wasn't food or anything else, just a good place to sleep and bathe.

It was in 1977 when I had worked the trials all day Saturday, and we would return for Sunday's trials. Saturday evening of this year's trials, one of the excise officers who lived near Indianapolis invited all of us to his condo for a get-together. It was something that, for me, was very enjoyable. We had some food and some beer and a lot of socializing with the guys who you hardly ever got to visit with. It was this particular evening though that will always stick with me as humorous.

Sgt. Pete Weiss, the officer who worked at headquarters, was amongst the officers there that evening. After hearing officers from all over the state talk about their experiences, or war stories, as police officers sometimes call them, Sergeant Weiss called attention for all of us to listen to this story he wanted tell us about that he said we'd all get a kick out of.

Pete told us about a phone call he had taken at headquarters one day from this crazy lady who owned a winery in the southern part of the state. My stomach started to rumble.

Pete said the lady called to complain about the excise police stopping her along a state highway with a roadblock, shotguns aimed at her, and flashing red lights. She was complaining that she was a respectful permittee of the Alcoholic Beverage Commission, and she thought she had been mistreated.

Sergeant Weiss continued telling this story as all the officers at the party were laughing. Pete said he told the lady she was sadly mistaken. He said he explained to her that excise police didn't have shotguns, didn't have red lights, and therefore didn't put up roadblocks along state highways for any reason. I'll never forget the laughter that came along with that tale. But it wasn't quite such a fallacy as being portrayed.

Yes, I did it. In sort of a way.

Here's what had happened. I had been traveling along a state highway one morning headed from home to the office at Madison. I came up upon this old hay wagon-looking truck that had farm license plates on it. The truck was about as loaded as it could be with whiskey barrels, and the smell of whiskey was strong in my car as I traveled behind the truck. I knew there was a chance these were empty whiskey barrels, but keeping in mind the strong smell was there, and I knew from experience that sometimes people took used whiskey barrels from a distillery and *sweated* the whiskey from the barrels. They'd wrap the barrel in plastic and set it out in the hot sun, and after a short time, they'd have this charcoal-colored, very strong tasting whiskey that could be drank.

I just traveled along for a few miles and thought what I wanted to know about what was really going on with this truck and all of its whiskey barrels leaving the Louisville area where distilleries were located. I was a little frustrated because we didn't have red lights to make such a traffic stop. But I did have a police two-way radio installed in a hidden place under my front seat. We didn't have radios either, but I had installed one without permission, and the Clark County Sheriff had assigned me the number 3A.

I was listening to that radio while I was behind this whiskey-barrel-ladened truck, with probably bogus farm license plates, and probably headed somewhere to *sweat* the whiskey out of those barrels for some illegal purpose.

I overheard on my two-way radio a couple of Clark County Sheriff's detective friends of mine headed in my direction. They were a few miles east of me headed toward me. After failing to locate a person wanted on an arrest warrant.

Since they didn't sound busy to me, I radioed them to see if they could stop this truck so I could investigate. They told me they would once the truck got closer to them, and I felt good with that. I was doing my job.

I followed the truck for almost another mile, and after coming around a bend in the highway, I came upon my detective friends. They had their unmarked detective car parked across the highway, with their flashing red light going to town, and they both were leaning over the hood of the car with their shotguns aimed at the approaching truck.

Well, to make it quick, I found out the driver was alone in the truck. The driver was a woman who owned a winery at Madison and was transporting some freshly emptied whiskey barrels she had purchased that morning to her winery to use as decorations.

Great story, Pete!

Taking Aim at Jeffersonville PD

The excise police experience was excellent, and I was learning more than I had ever imagined. On two separate occasions, the department created this special unit they called the Audit Staff, and I had been selected to be a member. The first time the unit was formed, we were told of specialized investigations we would be sent out on as a task force. We received quite a bit of training, but the unit was disbanded for a reason never told to me.

The second time this same unit was put together, a man who had been brought from another state agency began to organize it and told four of us, including me, that *we* were the actual *unit*, and he detailed the work we would be doing. It sounded fascinating, but within a few days, that unit was dissolved just like the first one.

And then, after three years with the excise police, a state senator introduced a bill to eliminate the entire Indiana State Excise Police Department and assign each county's sheriff to handle the duties. I thought, *Is this nuts or what?* I had a police job, and this job was protected under state law. Well, I quickly learned that the job I held was not protected by anything or anyone except for the chairman of the Indiana Alcoholic Beverage Commission. It was explained to me that if the chairman didn't like the way I combed my hair, he could send me packing without me having recourse. Man, what another lesson I learned. I hadn't had enough sense to know what I had myself get involved in for the past few years with this career, and I had set myself up for something, and I wasn't quite sure what. One thing I did quickly realize was that I am "getting outta here." I had this rude awakening that I was brought on by my own ignorance, and I was going to set myself straight and quite quickly.

I had expected to have a real police job. Such a job in the state of Indiana is protected, and you cannot just lose it for no good cause. I immediately applied for a job with the Jeffersonville Police Department. The department was taking applications, and I had arrived to apply at the right time.

I never told anyone at the excise police of my application. As far as I knew, they could dismiss me just for that.

My father passed away at the young age of fifty-four in the fall of 1977, just after I had applied for the Jeff Police job. Nearly all of the excise officers attended his funeral. My dad's coworkers at Jeff Police served as his pallbearers. I cannot remember being so emotionally touched as I was by the respect given to my father and me during this time. These were police officers making me feel this way.

During the visitation at Dad's funeral, my grandfather, Leonard Fleeman, led me up to a friend of his who lived near him as well. Grandpa told Guy Jackson that I was trying to get hired at Jeff Police and asked Guy to put a word in for me with the mayor. Grandpa and Guy were very much Republican, and the mayor, Richard Vissing, as well as almost the rest of the city, were Democrats.

I thanked Guy Jackson for anything he could do. He told me that Mayor Vissing *owed* him a favor and would say something to him. I knew he would. Guy Jackson and his children all lived near my grandparents, and I knew enough to know he was a man of his word.

Working for the excise police had been very enlightening. I had gained experience that I would be taking to another step in my career as a police officer. I had already said my goodbyes in my mind to the department and wished them well.

The department administration knew they had problems, and when you think about what hand of cards they had been dealt, they did pretty good. This was a department that had been previously made up of individuals who had been appointed to their jobs on strictly political reasons, and some were not trained as well as the younger officers being recruited and inserted into the ranks. Some of the older officers were retired from police departments, and they were worn out and not aggressive. These were the people in charge, for the most part.

Whenever I had went to Indianapolis to ABC offices to testify at a hearing, it was not unusual to run into officers from other parts of the state who were there for the same reason. I remember being called out on the high number of arrests and number of permittee violations we reported each month by some of these officers. Some of them were in charge of the district in which they worked and still were making these remarks. My district was considered the *armpit* of the state when it came to being assigned to a district with the excise police. You had to have lived in the district to appreciate the beauty and peacefulness of Southern Indiana, and these guys sure didn't seem to want any part of it, except for a short vacation with their family to a state park in the Southern Indiana area.

Instead, I heard guff from some of these officers about us making them look bad, and here I stood in my cheap sport coat, a cheap tie, wrinkled trousers, and worn dress shoes waiting to testify at a hearing. These guys from *up north* and from areas working the larger cities had expensive, smart-looking suits and shoes that I could never have thought about buying. They looked good. It made me think.

It did make me think about the *threat* that loomed over my employment in my home district. The *threat* of being transferred to a northernmost post as some sort of punishment or needed reassignment made me cringe to even think about it. I always kept that *threat* in mind when I did my job. I loved living close to home where my family was. The thought of having the option to have to move my home to some other part of the state for some simple reason or even having to live in a motel during the week on per diem and driving hours back and forth to visit my wife on my days off wasn't something I wanted to deal with.

There were two times during my venture with the excise police when I was told someone wanted me out of that district in Southern Indiana.

The first was when I was sent to investigate a Jeffersonville liquor store that was reportedly selling to minors. This wasn't *report-*

edly to me. It hadn't been but a few weeks earlier when my wife and I went there with another couple to buy some beer one Friday evening, so we could enjoy our trip to the Lakewood Drive-In Theater. I sat in the car while someone else bought our beer. The parking lot was full of minors loading booze into their cars. I knew all these kids. I was just in my early twenties, and the other couple with us was a year or two younger than me. This place was wide open, and everyone knew to go there and get *sold*. I knew not to initiate any action on my observations because the owner of this store was a very political person with a big family, and he was loved by everyone in town.

But the evening I received an assignment sheet to check out a complaint of this place, I knew it would be an easy task. The officer who was with me and I parked across the highway at a trailer park entrance and, within a minute or two, saw this 1968 Chevrolet Camaro pull up to the front door, and this obvious teenage boy who was driving entered the store and came out a few minutes later with beer and whatever else he had bought and began to put it in his trunk. We approached, ended up arresting the kid, and going inside the store to get the clerk who had made the sale identified.

The young man who was identified as the clerk was a friend of mine from high school. He and I used to drink his dad's beer when nobody else was at his house. And we were teenagers.

The owner of the store began yelling loudly at me over the crowded store making his point that I had singled him out and this was all political. I couldn't get out of that store quick enough. This is what they had warned me about being able to work in my home district.

The excise didn't arrest the permittees at the permit premises when this happened. We submitted case reports, and the ABC prosecutor would file administrative charges, usually ending up at a hearing and a fine of a couple of hundred dollars.

We took this eighteen-year-old boy from New Washington, Indiana, to a Justice of the Peace at Sellersburg, Indiana. The kid pled guilty and paid a fine, and we took him back to his car.

A hearing was held a couple of months later, and the store was fined. But this occurred after I received phone calls at home blasting me for what I had done, and I had even been pulled over by a Jeffersonville Police Officer while in my police car. This officer, whom I went to high school with, and had even drove him back and forth to the police academy when we both attended at the same time, also warned me about citing the store owner.

I had a relative who owned a liquor store just down the street from this store I am telling about. This relative actually was a second cousin to me, but I had always referred to him as Uncle. My uncle was president of the Clark County Package Store Association at the time.

One day after this incident dealing with the liquor store, I was at headquarters when Major Portolese called me in to his office. The major asked me if I knew this association president from Clark County, and I told him that I did. The major told me that this *Uncle* of mine had called him on behalf of the association and asked that I be transferred to the Evansville District. They didn't want me fired though, just moved away from Jeffersonville. Major Portolese didn't ask for any explanations about why an uncle of mine would do this. He knew the answers. He put his hand on my shoulder and told me to keep up the good work.

Then, at a time when I was already planning on leaving the department, Major Portolese called me in to his office once more. Again, he asked me about a complaint he had received. But this time, it was from a county prosecutor who didn't ask for my transfer but asked for me to be fired!

This stemmed from an incident almost a year earlier. It was a weekend evening, and three of us were assigned to work together. Since we were going to be in this one certain county, one of the officers asked if we'd mind stopping at this tavern in a small town to take care of an administrative task. Of course, we agreed. That wasn't a problem, and we went there.

When we arrived, I suggested that one of us stay outside, and the other two could go in and do whatever needed to be done. I suggested that because this is a place of business and we didn't ever have any complaints about how they ran the place, the three of us to enter might portray to the customers that the place was in trouble, being raided, or something else I didn't think we needed to say by our presence in force. I volunteered to stay outside.

It was a very nice evening, about 8:30 p.m. on a Friday evening. The tavern seemed busy, and I smelled food that I'd wished I could be sitting inside eating and drinking a cold beer.

It hadn't been but a couple of minutes until this car pulled up to the front of the tavern. There were three real pretty girls in the car, and they obviously were having a great time. They all had a cold beer, and a cooler was in the rear seat. They started talking with me and were just having a whole lot of fun. I stood out front of the tavern talking to them and found myself again thinking I'd wish I could be somewhere else that evening having some fun.

After talking to these girls, it seemed obvious they were intoxicated. This early in the evening, these girls who seemed eighteen or nineteen years old were drunk. I knew something would need to be done. I secretly hoped an adult who knew them would come out of this tavern and see what I saw and take the girls off the street. But instead, the other two officers I was with came out and asked me what was going on.

We arrested the girls, confiscated their alcoholic beverages, and drove them to the county jail. They were friendly, a little upset, but seemed to understand why we were doing what we're doing.

After booking them at the jail, one of the deputy sheriffs took me aside and clued me in on something. He told me that one of the girls was married to the county prosecutor's best friend, and one of the other girl's father was very involved in one of the political parties in the county. The deputy didn't know anything about the third girl.

We left that evening and went about our business as usual.

About a week later, I attended court in that county on a Saturday morning. The girls were scheduled to go to court that morning, and I was attending to represent the excise police and document whatever court findings there were. In smaller counties, they only had one court, and these misdemeanor charges were usually handled on these Saturday morning court sessions. This session was going to be in the county's circuit court.

The excise police had this policy, at least in our district, that if we could attend initial court appearances on anyone we arrested, we should. Plus, this will get me out of a weekend night's work. I'd just have to make up my time after I leave the court and find a way to get my eight hours in.

The courtroom was packed. It looked like fifty people would be dealt with. I didn't see but only one of the girls I had arrested in the room.

During a break, I was walking out in the hall when the county prosecutor saw me and came over to speak with me. He told me that in regard to the three girls I had arrested, one was his friend's wife and another's father was involved in the political party, and he would not be prosecuting those two girls. I really didn't care to see any of the girls have to deal with anything, but I was glad to have gotten them off the street before someone was hurt. I suggested to the prosecutor that he go ahead and let the third girl go, and he told me that he didn't know anything about her, and she would be prosecuted.

The court proceedings seemed long and boring as I sat and listened to the judge hand out punishment to a lot of people who, for the most part, were in court due to alcohol-related offenses. When the third girl I had arrested was called up, she ended up being *slammed* by the court. I thought it was harsh when the judge ordered her to some program in which she'd have to pay a few hundred dollars, and she did have a slight sentence tagged along with this program she had to attend.

I left court around noon. I felt a little sorry for this girl since the others weren't going to be charged, but I was trained to know one thing. The excise consider themselves *guests* in any county in which they work, and we should always keep that in mind. I just went on with my business as usual and tried to forget about the matter.

It was almost eight or nine months later when I walked into the district office in the late afternoon, having come in from a day out in the field. Upon entering, Sarge was there, having sat at his desk performing post duty that day as usual. Sarge told me that I had missed two telephone calls, and both of the callers said they'd call back. Sarge said one of these callers was the prosecutor of the county I am speaking about.

I thought I'd better call the prosecutor back to see what he needed. When I went to pick up the telephone to make the call, and before I could pick it up, it rang. I answered and found it was the person who also had called the office for me. It was the father of the third girl I had arrested, and the one who got prosecuted.

The man was very polite and said he needed to ask me a question. I told him to go ahead and ask, and he prefaced his question by telling me something. He said he knew the other two girls weren't prosecuted, and he understood why they weren't. He told me about their connections, and he explained his daughter wasn't *connected* with anything, and he had known that was why she was punished and the other two were not. His question to me was, "Why did you prosecute my daughter and let the other two girls go free?"

That was an excellent question, and I very much understood why he needed an answer. The man went on to say he had been prompted to call me for an answer since, in recent days, the other two girls had been driving past his home taunting his daughter because they got off, and she didn't.

I thought to myself that this is probably why the prosecutor had been calling for me.

I told this father that the excise police consider themselves guests in each county in which they work. I explained why we were in that county that evening when his daughter was arrested, and I told him why all three girls were arrested and what charges were filed by paperwork left by us at the jail that evening. I went on to explain that on the Saturday morning when his daughter appeared, it wasn't until the prosecutor told me he was deferring prosecution on the other two girls that I understood why they were not in court that morning. This man and I both knew the truth, but it wasn't my decision to turn those girls loose, and I wasn't lying to him. But this father politely told me he knew what the truth was, and he probably confirmed in his mind, by my lack of a response, and he flatly told me his daughter was prosecuted because she was not connected politically. I told him he should discuss the matter further with the prosecutor, and after some pleasantries, we hung up. I wasn't at all sure the man even believed a word I had told him.

I didn't wait a minute before I called the prosecutor at his office. His secretary told me he should be back from court soon, and she knew he wanted to speak with me. It wasn't but after a very few minutes when I received his return call.

The prosecutor thanked me for calling him back and immediately started to tell me that this girl's father would be calling me, and he needed to speak with me before I spoke with the man. I quickly told the prosecutor that I had just spoken with the girl's father. The prosecutor seemed surprised and asked me, "What did you tell him?" My exact response to him was, "I told him the truth."

Well, however I came across, or however this prosecutor heard my reply, things went south at that point. He started telling me I had caused him political trouble, and he couldn't believe I had told the father the truth. I tried to interject what I meant as stating "the truth," but it didn't matter. This prosecutor rattled on for a few moments, and we both hung up.

I told my sergeant and lieutenant about the entire matter, and it pretty well was dismissed as just another day in our line of work.

About a month later, the lieutenant and I met at a New Albany hotel restaurant with an Indiana State Police detective. We were going to be executing a search warrant that morning on a bootlegger, and we were going to eat breakfast first. I thought it was pretty cool that the only other people in the restaurant was this famous sixties' rock group that had performed the night before at a New Albany nightclub. I also thought it was cool that they were quietly sitting nearby, obviously interested in what we three cops were doing there. After all, we were plainclothes, had our guns somewhat visible, and we were talking police things.

I had done some undercover work on an investigation for this state detective in a nearby county where this prosecutor was located. I had given the detective my reports a couple of weeks earlier in order for him to file criminal charges. While eating breakfast, this detective told me he had went to that county to file his paperwork, and he was told by the prosecutor that he would not file anything with Jack Fleeman's name on it.

After explaining the entire matter, my lieutenant stated that we couldn't let this thing go, and we should meet with this prosecutor. That sounded good to me. I was trying to be a good police officer, and now I have an entire county in which I cannot work.

The following Monday, I did call the prosecutor and told him about our conversation with the state detective, and we wanted to meet with him. The prosecutor set up a meeting at his office a day later that week and advised me that the meeting would be tape-recorded. I agreed to that, and the meeting was set up.

My lieutenant was angry, to say the least, when I told him that the meeting would be recorded, and he told me he would be going with me, and we'd get this straightened out.

I actually was very much looking forward to this meeting. This needed to get straightened out, and I was sure it would be.

The lieutenant and I arrived at the prosecutor's office as scheduled, and the secretary made a call and told the prosecutor, "They're here." It was just a short time later when the prosecutor arrived and told us he'd be in just a moment. He went inside his office and shut his door. I figured he was setting up his tape recorder. That was fine with me. He came out a few minutes later and invited us inside his office. The lieutenant remained in his chair and told me, "I'll be right here. If you need me, just let me know." I stood up and looked at him in. What I am sure showed total pure disgust. I now knew exactly where I stood all of the way around this issue, and I was going in with a strong attitude. I also now fully realize exactly where I stood with this job.

I entered that office, and I did discuss the entire matter with the prosecutor. I listened to him complain that I had hurt him politically, and I affirmed that sometimes law enforcement officers, including a prosecutor, need to make hard decisions. That meeting lasted about forty-five minutes with one of the final comments from the prosecutor was him telling me that he would be calling my superiors and asked that I be fired.

I left the meeting and drove away from that county with my lieutenant. I was so consumed with the thoughts going through my mind. I understood why this small-time prosecutor acted this way, but how ashamed I was of my lieutenant. He and I hardly spoke during the drive back to my car in New Albany. We never discussed the matter again. I never worked in that county again either.

It was a few weeks later when Major Portolese told me about that prosecutor calling him and trying to get me fired from my job. His comments meant more to me than most could imagine. Looking back, he must have been through a lot himself. Later in life, I would take the lessons I had learned from him into my relationships with police officers I was trying to see prosper in their careers.

Perhaps that prosecutor succeeded with what he tried to accomplish. I left that job, but I didn't get fired as he had tried to get done. I already had my mind set that I was leaving, and that little moment outside his office was the factor that made me comfortable with my plans to make an exit.

I had always hoped that prosecutor learned from that incident. You need to be *on the ball* to become an attorney and even more to get elected to the job as prosecutor. I knew that these were small-time political situations, but that doesn't mean we cannot grow. I was learning, and I can only imagine this guy did as well. He is a judge now, and I am sure he must have learned a lot.

Joining the Jeffersonville Police

Chief Raymond Parker had called me to let me know I was being processed for employment with the Jeff Police. The chief always stayed in touch with me through the entire process, which lasted a couple of months.

I continued working for the excise police, but I was eagerly waiting for the moment I could leave.

Chief Parker told me I would need to take psychological exams, physicals, a polygraph examination, as well as a background investigation in order to proceed. I was willing and waiting.

Every time I was notified by the Jeffersonville Police to meet at the chief's office in order to file paperwork, pick up forms, or anything that I needed to meet about, I found something unusual was happening. There were two other men being processed for a job along with me. Each time I was told to be at the chief's office at such and such time for all of us to meet, I was always thirty minutes late. If the other applicants had been told to be there at 10:00 a.m., I was always told that I should be there at 10:30 a.m.

I knew what was happening, and the chief seemed to understand. Someone relaying the message to me wanted me to always be late, appearing to be a poor candidate for the job. I was late for everything. This went on through the entire hiring process. That is another story in itself.

Just before I was hired, I was at a weeklong advanced photography school at the Indiana Law Enforcement Academy.

When I finished the school and had gotten home on Friday evening, my wife told me the police department had called to tell me I was scheduled to appear before the Board of Police Commissioners. This would be the final step for me to take in order to be hired. I asked my wife when I was to appear, and she told me she had received a phone call from a detective telling her that I was to appear the following Monday evening at 7:00 p.m. But she said she received a subsequent call telling her that I was to appear Tuesday at 7:00 p.m. instead. I asked her if she was sure, and she said that's what she was told.

I was so excited. This was the final, major step to the career I truly wanted, and I was approaching the finish line.

I went to work for the excise police the following Monday. I was keeping my plans to myself, and I felt so many mixed emotions about what was going on in my career plans. And I couldn't tell anyone I was working with. I was looking at a couple of officers with so much disappointment, and the others all were wanting to leave the excise like I did. But you didn't want to say what you were doing. I was so much looking forward to Tuesday evening.

After the workday, I went with my wife to my grandparents' house for supper. Grandma always cooked big meals, and that's what I enjoyed. I had just left the table and sat on the couch to let the big meal start to digest when the telephone rang. The call was for me. The Jeffersonville Police Department chief of detectives was on the phone. I picked up the extension and was told in an urgent voice that I had been scheduled to appear at the Board of Police Commissioners at 7:00 p.m., and I was told to come straight to the Mayor's Office.

I probably seemed rude when I told my family I had to leave. I was pretty well upset. I thought here it is again. Throughout the entire hiring process, I had been late. I have always been a prompt person. But I was about forty-five minutes late for this meeting, and I was driving there being sure I would arrive soon since it was only a few blocks away, and I thought how good it was I was going to appear dressed right. I had been at work all day, and I had a sweater and tie on and looked good. I tried to keep a good attitude, and I felt something really *kick in* about myself. I knew deep down why I had been told to appear at a late time throughout this process, and I now knew why I was appearing before this board late again.

I arrived at the City-County Building and was met by the chief of detectives. Capt. Ron Kemp told me briefly how diligently he had been trying to find me. As he hurriedly walked me toward where I needed to go, I thanked him. He and I had worked together, and I knew him well. He wished me good luck. I always had hoped he had never had taken my last statement to him wrong. Before we parted ways, I told him that "I wanted his job." He and I both knew that would take years and he'd be retired and I'd have had to work for years to attain that position. But it felt really great just to say it.

When I arrived, the room seemed full, but I only saw the commissioners, Mayor Richard Vissing, and Chief Parker. There might have been a dozen others there, but I was focused on them.

I was immediately called up before the board. Before I was asked any questions, I told the board that I was sorry for being late. I explained the mix-up, and I told the board that all through the process there had been a few similar mix-ups, and they seemed to understand.

I proudly stood before that board and answered their questions. A few comments were made by a couple of commissioners and then Mayor Vissing made a comment. He told me that after careful consideration, he knew that Guy Jackson was right. I smiled at the mayor, and I thanked him. I was so overwhelmed that the mayor had made that comment. It took me back to the thoughts of my father's funeral, the love of my family, and the love of friends.

I left shortly after that and went home.

The very next morning, Chief Parker called me at home. He told me I did well in my appearance at the meeting, and the commissioners had recommended that I be hired. The chief told me I had the job. He said I would start work March 1. That was in 1978.

I immediately gave written notice to the excise police about my resignation in order to go to work at Jeff. I actually would be starting work before two weeks would be up, but I had some vacation time I would need to take, and that all worked out fine. This meant I had four or five days to work with the excise before leaving.

The final day would involve me going to headquarters at Indianapolis and turning my car, gun, badge, and other issued equipment in. There was some paperwork that would need to be filled out as well.

But the next to last day involved a trial I would need to appear at in Connersville. There was a guy who Sarge and I had arrested for public intoxication, and he and I both would need to testify in court at a morning bench trial. This was a city court and the judge would decide guilt and it should go smooth. I sure wanted it to be finalized that day so I wouldn't have to come back.

Sarge and I did testify that morning, and the guy was found guilty. I never understood the reason he took it to trial, but I figured he might have been on probation or had a suspended sentence hanging over his head and had hoped for an acquittal.

Sarge drove that morning, and when the trial was over and we were leaving Connersville, he told me he wanted to buy me lunch since I was leaving the job. He told me he was taking me to Miller's at North Vernon. This was a place that did have an alcoholic beverage permit and was known mostly as a place that served really good food. I'd heard about it all the time I worked for the excise and especially when I was in North Vernon. Going there for lunch sounded great except for one thing. Miller's was known amongst the excise officers to be a *pop stop*. This tavern in downtown North Vernon was known for good food, and I didn't ever remember hearing a complaint about the place. But they treated excise too nice as far as us younger officers felt. We avoided pop stops to avoid an appearance of favoritism. There were times during this stint with the excise I found myself going with a senior officer to a pop stop in a couple of different cities in our district, and I had found a way to allow myself to tolerate these free meals and drinks whenever one of the situations arose. I always made myself feel comfortable by leaving the money for my meal and tip on the table and just let it look like I was a great tipper.

When he had said we were going to Miller's, I reminded Sarge about how I felt about pop stops, and he looked sternly at me and stated, "I'm buying your lunch." He and I both knew where each other was coming from, and I replied to him as I usually did and said, "And I'm leaving a big tip".

Privately, I was really going to enjoy this lunch. Like I said, I had always heard about the good food, and that's one of my favorite things to do, eat good food! And after all, I am leaving this pop stop department tomorrow, and I shouldn't care what anyone thought about me sitting in a joint eating and drinking free like a sloth. But I had my principles, and that type of behavior wasn't on my life's agenda.

We arrived at Miller's right at lunchtime, and the place was busy. Sarge and I sat in a booth in the barroom. I knew what I was ordering as soon as I saw it on the menu. I ordered the Reuben sandwich, and I was going to put some of that awesome-looking beer mustard they had on the bar on my sandwich. I had seen beer mustard at so many bars I had visited when checking permits and had tried making it myself. Miller's had beer mustard in a clear glass jar, and I could see these red speckles in the mustard telling me it might be hot and spicy, just what I like!

The owner of the business recognized Sarge a short time after we sat down. He stood at the end of our booth talking with Sarge, and I didn't care to pay any attention to what they talked about because I was going to enjoy this sandwich with this hot beer mustard. This place had some of the best iced tea as well. I thought maybe everything tasted so great because I was secretly celebrating inside, and this was part of the fun.

While Sarge and the owner talked, our food had arrived. I started this celebration of food I had missed over these past few years. My celebration quickly became a mixed bag of emotion. I regretted I let my principles keep me from enjoying a great sandwich like this, but I was starting this new job in a few days, and I could always come back!

The rest of this little lunch story is like something out of a movie. Three decades later, I still cannot believe it happened. I have always believed this happened because there was a reason.

While Sarge talked and I ate, there was this old man who entered the bar, and he immediately recognized Sarge and came up to our booth to say hello. Sarge looked at the man and told him, "Sir, I'm sorry, but do I know you?" The man told Sarge his name, and Sarge immediately apologized to him for not recognizing him. The man told Sarge he was sick and was taking treatments that were wearing him down. Sarge got up from the booth and invited the man to sit with us. This older gentleman slid in and was sitting right across from me while Sarge continued speaking with the owner of Miller's.

This gentleman asked me if I worked with Sarge, and I told him I did. He asked if I was new, and instead of going into a lot of details, I just said yes.

The man then told me he had known Sarge for a long time when he was a bartender down the street at the Nip 'n' Sip. Now I recognized this man too.

He was the bartender on that first assignment Sarge had sent Phil and I to four years earlier on that complaint of gambling. I was going to hear something from this man that I never expected, and it was going to be something to change my life in several ways about how I felt about myself and how I did my job.

This man told me that one afternoon a few years ago, Sarge sent a couple of new officers into the Nip 'n' Sip for him to keep an eye on and to report back on how they performed. I quickly now understood that this is why I felt paranoid that day, and this is also why that paranoia haunted me every time I worked undercover. Having been through many interesting lessons so far with this job, I had to know one thing from this man, and I asked him, "How'd they do?" This guy said, "They did okay"

I didn't comment when this man told me this. I had so much anger inside me that I really wanted to get up and walk away from Sarge and this whole operation. I didn't have a car there and didn't know how in the world I would get home, so I stuck it out. I finished that lunch, felt indigestion coming on, and put a wad of bills on the table when we left.

I never said a word to Sarge about what I had just learned nor did I ever say a word about this to Phil. Actually, I cannot remember ever seeing Phil again while working as an excise officer. I do know that it was within a couple of weeks he left the department also. He returned to the Indiana University Police Department at Bloomington. He would later become chief of the Indiana University Southeast Police Department in New Albany.

I couldn't get this job over quick enough. I decided that this was going to be another lesson to take with me through my hopefully long journey ahead of me in police work.

All of my life, it seemed I knew the day would come when I would become a Jeff cop. It is what I dreamt about, hoped for, planned for, and, in my own sort of way, had trained myself for.

I didn't just dream of being a cop. I wanted to be a good police officer, set examples, learn as much as I could while on the job, and most of all, attain the position of detective.

I had used every experience I had encountered to apply to this training. I wasn't very much for watching police shows on television and drawing conclusions on how police should perform.

A few years before I had been hired by the excise, I read a book that was published concerning a report by a task force President Johnson had set forth to examine police and the work they do. This task force arose after the 1968 Democratic Convention in Chicago. The police were involved in many violent situations, and I will always remember reading a news account calling it a "riot by police."

That book contained what I considered good things to know if I wanted to be a good officer. I must have read that book ten times. The very most important thing I drew from that book, and still hold on to nearly four decades later, is that police officers should try to live normal lives when away from the job. The task force recommended officers to socialize more with civilians. This was to help the officers to stay in touch with what the general community feels, and think how their police should be responding. I have always seen that this is very important. I have seen some police officers shield themselves from anyone who wasn't a police officer. I understand why, but I wouldn't know how to, at this time and day, to try to explain the reasoning to young officers. It needs to be explained to them early on like I taught myself.

But now I am preparing to embark on my life's dream. This is going to be my career. This is what I have always wanted. I won't be rich, at least when you speak about my paycheck. I knew I didn't need that. I grew up very happy and comfortable, and if that is what I knew and enjoyed, then that is my paradise!

One thing I never anticipated was being a police officer at another department before I became a Jeff cop. This is a plus, I thought. I have so very much experience to bring to the department that most officers who have retired from there never had.

I had received much training, worked all over the state of Indiana, worked with many different law enforcement agencies, conducted raids, prepared many search warrants, and executed them. I had handled evidence, made new releases, made hundreds of arrests, worked undercover, and just dealt with so many situations I could go on for a year explaining what they were and how I learned from them. That is what it is all about. Learning from it. You need to take each and every experience and grow from it. It doesn't matter if you were right or wrong, it is that you did the best you could, drawing from what you knew, and whatever the outcome, learned from the whole thing. And then you are a little bit better prepared for the next one.

But here I come, Jeffersonville Police Department, and I am bringing all of Jack Fleeman to the job.

I knew there were a couple of obstacles that I may or may not have to deal with when I arrive. You see, Jeffersonville is a river town, along the Ohio River and right across a bridge from Louisville, Kentucky. Whether you know the history or not, the one thing for sure was that the Jeff Police had a history that wasn't too impressive when it came to some things that were in the past.

Gambling was a major part of the city in the years before. There were gambling joint all through the county, and police just looked the other way. I had asked my dad once if he knew anything about a story I had heard about the city police. I told him that I had heard stories about Jeff police officers *rolling* drunken sailors who had come to town to gamble. Dad told me the story. The sailors were in town for training and routinely came to Jeffersonville to party. Everything they wanted was there. When one of them got u unruly and the police were called, they might have been *rolled* of their money. I asked Dad if he had ever done this, and he told me a story. He said that shortly after being hired, he and his partner went to one of the downtown joints and arrested a drunk sailor. He explained he was working second shift, and they had just came on duty when they made the arrest. Dad said that after booking the drunk into jail, they resumed patrol, and while driving east on Tenth Street, Dad saw his partner counting a wad of money. My dad told me he asked where that had come from, and his partner told him he had taken it off the drunk they had just arrested. I asked Dad if he took any of the money, and he quickly said no. He and I never discussed the incident again, ever.

Knowing what I knew at this point, I would have understood if Dad had said yes. He knew I was really listening and the reasons I was listening, and I hope his answer was the truth.

But that's really all right if it wasn't. I want to start now and try to do whatever I can to change things. I want to make the place better than how I found it. At least I intend to do what I can toward that effort.

The Jeff Police had hired several young men and a couple of women in the few years before I was being brought onboard. I knew most of them. They were really good people and would bring good things with them as they did their jobs.

I knew getting hired at Jeff had been more of a chore that the others who were also being processed may have experienced. With being a half-hour late for every interview, physical, or whatever, and almost a full day short for my final interview with the commissioners. It hadn't been but three weeks earlier when a couple of Jeff cops stopped me on Court Avenue near headquarters. One of the officers, a sergeant, told me he had heard that I was soon to be hired. I told him that I had my fingers crossed. He commented that the department really needed someone with the knowledge I had to enforce some of these ABC laws, and he was really glad I was coming. I knew he was full of crap. I knew him, probably more than he could imagine. I thanked him, and he rode off with his partner. I watched as they drove out of sight, but not like into the sunset. I watched him go about a block, and in his side-view mirror, I saw him slap his knee and laugh. I had been paying attention. This is one thing my father taught me. I enjoyed learning anything that would help me progress in this new job!

It was almost eighteen years later at the Jeff Police that I actually witnessed something happen to an applicant that had happened to me. I was involved in the department's administrative process in hiring, and I got to see something that confirmed my feelings.

I actually witnessed a high-ranking officer, who had been trained under the guidance of the same commander who I always had known had sent me to those meetings a half-hour late and probably to my interview a day late, tell an applicant when to show up for his interview. This high-ranking man didn't like this applicant's now-retired officer's kin, and he made no bones about it. This applicant, a fine young man, was told his interview to become a Jeffersonville Police Officer was next Friday at 3:00 p.m. I hadn't heard anything, but this young man was scheduled for Tuesday at 3:00 p.m. I was so disappointed when he didn't show up for that Tuesday interview. I had said so many good things about him. But Friday, while leaving work, here he came, in his suit, ready for his interview. I saw him in the parking lot. I told him he was late, and he was a few days late. He was so certain I was mistaken and he was on schedule that he walked past me to this interview. It wasn't going to happen as everyone had went home. He did get a rescheduled interview, and he did get hired. I knew what he went up against, but instead of feeding that idea, I thought best to let that die, and I never discussed with him what I had witnessed happen to him.

Like that day at Miller's, learn from it. Like that liquor store in Jeff I busted for selling beer to minors, learn from it.

My first day at Jeff Police began at 8:00 a.m., March 1, 1978. I had been hired along with a guy I had went to high school with, and we both started the same day. I wore plain clothes since they have to take me to the uniform store and get me fitted.

One of the best pieces of information I received as I became a Jeffersonville Police Officer came from several people who wished me well. They were retired Jeff cops, present Jeff cops, and officers from other departments. This tip, they all seemed to know well and wanted me to fully understand, was to keep your mouth shut. This wasn't a tip for me not to tell about things I saw, but to listen and learn. I was used to that. My father had taught me that early in life, and I prepared myself to do exactly that.

The first few days went slow. I didn't have a gun or a uniform, and I was just riding in the back seat of a two-man car. The department was a far cry from any more but dreaming about everybody having their own police car. We had about seven police cars to patrol in. You could count on a couple of them being broken down at any given time. You'd have to think about it. Here we have a full-sized police car equipped that ran twenty-four hours a day, seven days a week. At least we did have air-conditioning when it worked.

The city didn't buy cars with even an AM radio in it. The city council wouldn't have heard of it. So, part of your equipment you always had was your trusty AM and maybe FM radio that you could stick up on the dashboard. You had to have it there so the antenna could be extended to pick up a signal. Also, you had to consider how to run the extended antenna through the wiring that stuck out of the spotlight to keep the radio in place. I lost more than a few radios driving "code 3" only to watch my radio bust loose and fly out the opened car window. The windows were always down because the air-conditioning seldomly worked

I returned to the scene of the "fly out" a couple of times to pay respect to my faithful radio. I couldn't believe what a beating they took. The plastic things were usually smashed to smithereens. It was the cost of trying to be entertained while at work. I learned to tie them down better when I started to receive cheap radios as birthday and Christmas gifts. When you were off-duty, you always tucked them away with your ticket book, notepad, or other essentials in your briefcase.

Try this, lay a cheap radio on your dashboard with all windows down. Now drive like a maniac, turning left, right, over here and down there, and see if your radio doesn't flop around a little. We were in the business, and ours literally flew out the window routinely. It was part of the job!

We wore police hats then as well. I always resented it when a nonpoliceman called them bus driver hats. I thought they looked good. But you could only lay them topside down on the dirty, vinyl back seat, next of your briefcase when you rode in a two-man car. Those hats slid everywhere and were always filthy.

We were issued shotguns that had stocks that folded up. They were cool. AC Upholstery made us all customized carrying cases to keep them in. It always seemed to feel like we were carrying a tommy gun or something else pretty unique when you carried the gun to the car and back into the station at the end of a shift. I didn't get it out too many times.

I was getting into this job now, and I was eager to get to the action. I was issued my uniform. It had all the removable parts you'd ever want to deal with on anything. But I was sure to polish each *P* button, my whistle chain, my JPDs that fit on my collar, and the name tag which also had the year I started—1978. I polished that badge most of all carefully not to rub the gold paint off and especially mess up the lettering and my badge number 119. The first day on the job, I learned you could buy this special polish called semichrome at the local hardware store, and it was the best you could use to shine things up. I think that one tube I bought lasted three or four years. After a while, you get over that stuff. A damp towel on the shiny leather and maybe a little home polish on the shoes worked just fine. After not polishing those buttons for a year, I noticed they looked just fine.

I had never worn a police uniform before, and this felt different. I was proud, very proud, but I felt uncomfortable when everyone looked at me. When they addressed you, they always seemed to look at that part of my nameplate that read Serving Since 1978. I always felt that meant "serving since today."

When 1979 rolled around, I had some time under my belt, and I was losing my *rookiness*, and those choosing to read my nameplate would know it!

After starting work as a uniformed officer, I soon realized that I was going to witness things I had only heard about and most nonpolice people refused to think about.

I saw distraught citizens after they had come home from work to find their homes ransacked and their belongings stolen. I dealt

78

with family members going to check on shut-ins, including their own family members to find that they had died a day or so earlier. I would sometimes stand alone in the rooms where these deceased people laid and thought what their last moments must have been like. I saw people dead who were found sitting on the toilet, sitting on a chair watching television, and lying in bed as they had went to sleep. I had also found people who took shotguns to their head and brains were splattered everywhere, stuck pistols in their mouths to end it that way, overdosed on pills and booze, and hanging themselves in their homes to quietly end it all. I dealt with an individual, in his nineties, who ended it all that way after leaving friends and relatives several notes on his dining room table.

Store clerks never seemed to be as upset as I ever imagined when I would be the first person to arrive after they had been robbed at gunpoint. Some of them were more experienced in being robbed that I was in trying to deal with it in the correct way.

I routinely escorted men from their homes after having domestic disputes with their wives, or whomever, only to be back the next day. This especially upset me when it was clear the man had injured the woman. It seemed the men were always back by the end of shift. We had to have arrested them for whatever charge. We didn't have the domestic violence charges to use then that came around later. It was so surreal for me to see a beaten woman standing outside the jail, waiting to meet the bondsman she had called to bail her man out. I later realized the reasons they were there, and I also understood why the new laws came into effect to help these women who really had nowhere else to turn.

The Center for Women and Families eventually came into the scene after the Rape Relief Center ran its course. That organization may still be around, but I think that many of the issues are now being handled by the center. Early on, I had met many victims of domestic violence and sexual abuse who would arrive at emergency rooms to assist victims as they worked as volunteer counselors to help these victims. I was initially upset when I started to deal with these advocates because they questioned what actions the police had taken. I always tried to keep my true feelings out and to keep my mind open

365

797576379325862573925

to try to learn why they questioned the police so much. Now, we receive routine training about why police officers need to understand why such questions are posed. We needed that change for sure.

Pursuits were always the maximum fun in my early years. I didn't know enough to care about liabilities back then. I was just doing my job with the tools they gave me to do it with. I chased many cars and motorcycles who had committed anything from driving recklessly, robbing a store, stealing the car they were in, having hurt somebody, and one time I chased some guy who wrecked, and we never figured out why he ran. We thought he was a fugitive child molester from Florida, but it wasn't him. That guy's elbow bone stuck out his arm after he rammed that tree. I caught that molester from Florida a few hours later.

I can't remember the many high-speed chases I had. Near collisions, near pedestrians being run over, bad accidents, trucks flipping over, foot chases after the bad guys bailed, lots of property damage, plenty of pain, and plenty of arrests and convictions fed into the excitement. Years later, as a supervisor, I would cringe when a chase started. I learned to pick up my microphone and terminate them (spoilsport).

When I was hired, we didn't have one-man police cars; we rode around in pairs. However, supervisors usually rode by themselves though.

Initially, none of us had portable two-way radios. Usually those were called walkie-talkies back then. The city didn't have the money to furnish them, so we relied on the two-way radio in the police car and remembering a story of a Louisville police officer, I always tried to keep some change in my pocket for a pay phone. It was a dime to make a call then.

It seemed it was always on night shift when I would be in a situation where I was wishing I had a radio to call for help. We would get these calls, like a prowler, and my partner and I would split up. Every once in a while, I would see the guy and get in a foot chase. I might have chased this idiot a block or two, and there was no way in heck that my partner even knew I was chasing someone. Usually it was after I tackled his ass and was fighting him, when someone would yell out their window, "What's going on out there?" I found myself actually getting into these type of situations and expecting to hear a neighbor yell out like that. I would merely yell back, "Police officer, call the police station and send me help." That always worked. One night, that exact thing happened, and one of the officers told me later that he had heard me screaming at the man I was fighting and knew to get there quickly. He was right. I was about worn out on that one. I always kept in mind that I had a home to go to after work and not let any of these idiots keep that from happening.

You were always so grateful when help arrived. There were a few times I did go home, but by way of the emergency room. Just an x-ray or an ice pack was what I usually needed, but one time I had an ankle brace for a couple of months.

Being a *rookie* had its price. Aside from being the last on the list to pick when you wanted to take a vacation or get about anything, you were always at the top of the list when it came to work parking meters. Jeffersonville had these meters all over downtown that only cost pennies to use. If you let the meter expire, you'd get a parking ticket. The fine was a whopping quarter, that is if you paid in a timely fashion. If not, you got hit for a dollar!

The idea for the parking meters was to keep people from parking all day in front of businesses and keeping store customers away since they wouldn't be able to park close. Enforcing the meters cost some dollars, but it was figured the return would be greater.

The police department's job was to keep parking violators in check. The younger officers worked on a rotating schedule, and whoever the lucky person was got to write tickets that day. You were expected to write a book full each shift. The only neat thing about this duty was you drove a three-wheeled motorcycle. The department had a three-wheeled Harley Davidson equipped with this little siren that ran by rubbing against the front tire, and a small red light was affixed on the front of the cycle. The day did come when the motorcycle was traded in, and the department moved up to this new vehicle. It was another three-wheeler, but this one was like a telephone booth on wheels. At least it seemed like a telephone booth that we used to have on street corners, and it had a driver's seat, a steering wheel, and windshield wipers. I guess if they wanted tickets written when it rained, we'd get it done!

Sunday mornings were even more humiliating for the young, up-and-coming police officer. You would have a hard time impressing even your best of friends when you had to go out early on Sunday mornings and empty the parking meters. You needed to push this metal container on wheels all over downtown and use a key to open the meters and empty them. That took a couple of hours. And on Monday mornings, you had to count that load of coins. At least I was in a basement area where nobody could see this future *forensic expert* counting pennies. When you were finished, you didn't seem so unimportant when you carried the bags of coins into the bank for deposit. After all, I might have been returning coins stolen in a robbery or something just as police-like!

I was so caught up in this job. I loved everything about it.

I was off-duty one night, around seven in the evening. I was headed to meet my friend Bill Temple at Federal Security's office at the Medical Arts Building. Bill is the one who had hired me when I was younger and given me experience working in security and dealing with burglar alarm sales. He had also given me a two-way radio to keep in touch with him, and I also could talk with Jeff Police on this radio. I did have permission to have this radio.

On this evening, I overheard officers being sent to a house at Eighth and Pratt Streets to investigate a man having been shot in the face. The dispatcher was telling officers the suspect was walking north on Pratt Street toward Ninth Street. I heard the officers who were out there tell the dispatcher their locations, and that they were headed toward the area. I immediately got excited thinking that if this was happening on day shift, I could deal with this shooting, but we changed shifts every month, and I wasn't on duty. I was going to miss out on this action.

It was a split second until it dawned on me, and I then realized I am a block away from where the suspect was headed, and I am a police officer twenty-four hours a day. I am going for it!

I was driving a pickup truck, and I did have my issued Smith and Wesson .357 revolver stuck in my shoulder holster at the time.

I followed my instinct and turned toward where the suspect had last been seen. And there he was! It was a guy I had went to school with, and he was quickly walking away from the scene. I thought, *Oh my gosh, here I am, and here I go!*

I pulled up slowly in my truck next to this guy while he was just outside my driver side window, and I said, "Hey, how's it going?" I never thought he ever recognized me there at that moment in the darkness. But he asked me, "How about a ride downtown?" I told him, "Sure, get in on the other side." I was instantly grabbing the microphone to that two-way radio telling the dispatcher that I had the suspect at Ninth and Fulton Streets. I threw the microphone down and stepped out of my truck. I pulled that revolver out and pointed it at him, telling him to put his hands up. I was so ever thankful that when he stuck those hands way up into the air, I saw a pistol in his waistband. *Whew*, I thought, *I got this one right!*

The officers on duty took him to jail. The guy who had been shot lived to tell what had happened. The guy I had caught had went to his house to borrow some money, and when he refused, the guy shot him square in the face. After that evening, I never heard one word about how I caught that guy. I thought I might be thinking selfishly when I thought someone might have at least said "good job." But that never happened. After some time, and after getting over my feelings of being ignored, I realized that this is the job. What I had done might have been something new and exciting for me, but it was expected of me, and it would be something that I would find myself doing many times again.

For the next couple of years, when I worked day shift, I regularly saw that guy's wife drag all their kids and push a grocery cart full of laundry down Watt Street to a laundromat. I had went to school with her husband, and I had sent those children's father to prison, and I wanted very much to ask her how he was doing. I never did. I never knew how much time he received, but after some years, when he got out, he and I were fine. He and I talk even to this day even though I rarely see him. Those kids would later cause him grief as they matured, got involved in relationships he didn't approve of, and I was sometimes the police officer called to help him find one of them or chase off one of their boyfriends. He seemed to have very good values. He knew how outside influences could affect their lives, like those influences affected his life, and he was genuinely concerned. He was always feeling so helpless and frustrated. I guess he and the children's mother were divorced or he just wasn't in their mom's life anymore, and he wasn't in their home.

Rotating Shifts

The shift work was probably the hardest thing about this job. We would work a month on days, 6:00 a.m. to 2:00 p.m., and then go to night shift, 10:00 p.m. to 6:00 a.m., and then to afternoon shift, 2:00 p.m. to 10:00 p.m. Once you got adjusted to a shift, it was time to change again. We actually had to report to work fifteen minutes before shift began. We usually just arrived in time to get our brief-cases, shotguns, and night sticks out of our lockers, and we just sat in a squad room and waited until we could hear the shift going off-duty go out the door. We would then walk out to the front area of the station, and we read on either the blotter, or a piece of paper on the radio console, who we were assigned to ride with and in which car. Some of the seasoned officers, those who had been on the department a year or so, seemed to enjoy having a new guy like me to ride with and learn from them. But a couple of the officers looked at us as a burden, and you knew it by their attitude, even though they didn't actually say it.

The way the schedule ran at the end of night shift, you all got this one night off *free*. It was a night when all of the officers were off-duty and didn't report back until the next afternoon. This night off was a traditional night of partying. You soon came to realize this one night off helped you decompress. That is a term that none of us knew then, but we were doing it. Alcohol was always a part of it.

On these "shift change" events, you would do the partying, and you always found it a time to reflect back to a rough time that previous month and express gratitude to a couple of officers and to finally thank them for saving your ass. I never actually heard any verbal expressions of any of that, but we all knew what was happening. Of course, those officers had similar gratitude to extend as well. We all took care of each other. The conversations we had may have been no more than a mere mention of your appreciation or thanking an officer for just showing up when he did on some call you had made.

Day shift was usually not very exciting to a young officer. Since we drove line cars, those few 24/7 cars were always needing maintenance, washing, and some downtime getting those things done. The police department needed errands taken care of as well. The local printer was always a visit you made to pick up some forms, the state police post was a source of forms as well as breathalyzer tubes, and the radio shop was also visited during the morning hours. With those errands and the normal calls you would get, the shift ran quick, but not too exciting. Normal calls were businesses and car owners reporting their place had been broken into overnight, and things had been stolen. There usually wasn't much excitement on day shift. That's what the younger officers lived for.

Second shift was busy: car accidents, domestic disputes, theft reports, drunks, suspicious people, fights, and neighborhood squabbles were the norm. Taking calls was never a problem. The problem was taking the calls and having enough backup to be sure everyone stays safe. As the city has grown and the police become busier, things never seem to improve.

Third shift was totally different. You patrolled businesses looking for burglars. It became an art to shine that spotlight on a door and be able to see if the door was locked or not. You familiarized yourselves with businesses, and you knew who kept what lights on and who didn't. It was very nerve-wracking to watch the city over the nighttime hours and go home believing you left things secure just to return the following night to find you were ripped off all over town. I found it upsetting when I checked all of my businesses thoroughly in my district, and once I left the area, an officer calls in a burglary in progress at the last place you had checked. It was almost humiliating to me. I wanted to catch that burglar, and it was obvious to me that once he saw me patrol by, checking the place out thoroughly, he *hit* it. I later got to know a lot of burglars, and that is how some of them worked. They watched the target, saw the police car pass, and thought we were on some schedule, and there was a time they would be safe to break in. To me, it became a game of cat and mouse. They were the mouse, and I was the cat.

One night I had just checked a drugstore then drove a block or two and then heard the dispatcher radio to all of us that a silent burglar alarm was going off at the same drug store. My partner and I arrived within seconds and found the front door glass shattered, and pieces of glass still *dripping* onto the sidewalk. We surrounded the place, thoroughly checked the inside of the store, and found the burglar was gone. There were no witnesses, and after a while, the pharmacist arrived to tell us what drugs were missing. Several years later, the burglar and I actually met. He told me that after he had seen the police car pass, his girlfriend drove him up to the front door. He told me he had a piece of concrete block already with him, and he threw it through the front door. He estimated he wasn't in the store a minute when he ran back outside, crossed the busy street, and ran to his car at a shopping center where he and his girlfriend lay down in the car for about fifteen minutes. Once they saw they could slide away, they did. This is part of what has made my job exciting. It took a few years, but another lesson learned.

Car accidents were something we all worked routinely on first and second shifts. I have seen cars split in half and the occupants walk away, and I have seen a carload of people in a taxicab run over by a bus.

I went to this one accident that had happened a few feet outside the city limits, and the sheriff's department was working the accident. I went there to assist in any way. This car had collided with a motorcycle driven by this guy and a girl he had invited to ride with him. The girl had a severe head injury and was laying on the pavement. I had arrived just moments after the accident had happened, and I was the first person to tend to her. She didn't have any significant bleeding, but she had a grapefruit-sized swelling on the side of her head. I held her head still and tried to keep her from moving until the ambulance arrived. I will always have the memory of this nineteen-year-old black-haired girl whimpering, "Momma...Momma," before she seemed to stop breathing. It was then the ambulance arrived and took her to the hospital where she was pronounced dead. This is one of the types of stresses I later learned about that causes police officers problems.

Third shift is also when fights broke out. It would normally be at a bar when you'd get such a call. It would also be normal that when the police arrived, the fight suddenly stopped, and after entering the bar, you had to figure out who was going to jail. My size was always my advantage when bar fights broke out, and when I arrived first and alone, I knew it wasn't just out of respect for the police that the fight suddenly stopped. After some time on the job, I knew most everybody who frequented bars and got into trouble, and they knew me. It was that fact that always seemed to help me resolve many arguments between these drunks. I knew that my relationships with them helped all of us. My dad taught me that, and I always thought about what he had taught me when I would be in the middle of a bar fight. I knew one thing, not everyone with alcohol on their breath needed to go to jail.

There was this one night that also will stay with me. I was riding along with another officer, and we were at the police station when a call came in about a shooting that had just occurred in a pretty nice neighborhood in town.

My partner and I were the first ones to arrive. My partner knew the man who lived there, and he had just shot a man several times in the front of his house. I knew the man who had been shot. He was lying in the front yard struggling to breathe. He had bullet holes in his body that were bleeding profusely. My experience working at the hospital and my EMT training were falling into play very quickly. I used my fingers to plug the bullet holes. That seemed to work except for that one hole under his thick leather belt that I had trouble getting to.

I knew the situation was under control as my partner had the guy who did the shooting under control, and I could hear sirens getting closer. I recognized the police sirens, but I also heard the siren of the ambulance I so wanted there.

Time seemed running in slow motion as I tried to keep my old friend from dying. He and I had been friends since junior high school. Like most school friends, we all went different ways. While I became a police officer, he joined a motorcycle gang. I had my ideas why he had chosen to go that route, and that was fine with me. I knew he was still the good guy I had always known even while he belonged to this club. Every year, he and another police officer had been going to Maine to visit a friend and go *lobstering*. I had been sworn to secrecy on that one. If any of the other gang members had suspicioned he was frequenting with the police, he wouldn't have survived.

I yelled for my friend to hang in there. I yelled louder and louder as sirens got closer. When he took that one, long, sigh-like breath, I knew he was gone. He had died while I was holding him.

The two guys had met earlier at a bar and had several drinks. They decided to go to one of the men's home, and my friend apparently got way out of line when he began making sexual suggestions to the other guy about what would happen when that guy's wife arrived home.

You didn't have to work many car accidents on third shift. The ones you did work usually involved a drunk driver.

After one really bad shift on nights, I arrived home shortly after 6:00 a.m. I had seen some horrible things that night with people's behavior and the filth that they lived in. As soon as I stepped foot inside my house, I got down on my knees and kissed my floor. And that was dirty green shag carpet right inside the front door, the dirtiest spot in the house. I so much appreciated my home, my life, and being home. Anytime that I tried to explain that quiet moment, people looked at me like I was weird. Nobody realizes what police deal with unless they have walked in those shoes.

I always strived to be a good officer. I tried to set a good example, especially to new officers. It really makes me feel good to tell people how I tried to teach officers that when they deal with the public. In good or bad situations, you need to *kill them with kindness*.

That tidbit only went so far. Sometimes you would try that technique, but sometimes situations would go south, and you found yourself needing to switch gears and become someone you might have chosen not to otherwise become. Like being a stern officer and needing to raise your voice and try to make someone try to understand that they may need to change their behavior, let that neighbor legally park his car in front of his house, perhaps keep that dog of theirs quiet at night and not let all that barking keep the neighborhood awake. You might need to take a deaf ear when they try to tell you that their prize pet is loving and wouldn't hurt anyone and just tell them they might get a citation if *Fido* isn't kept inside or quiet. You might need to explain to some citizens that their kids aren't really angels, and they might be eligible to be taken to the juvenile authorities if things were not corrected with their behavior when away from home. And sometimes you might need to put that deep tone in your voice to try to make someone understand that even though you understand that they might need the money, but they cannot work on cars out on the street, night after night, day after day, running a repair business out in front of their neighbor's property. You might have to know a few city ordinances to make your point.

Perhaps you needed to take a stronger than normal approach when you had to explain, or just plain tell someone, maybe even one your own friends, that the neighbors really don't want to hear their loud music when they entertain their friends and are trying to have a good time. And sometimes, yes, we do have more important things we need to be doing.

And sometimes after killing them with kindness and piece of advice went out the window a long time ago, you have to just go ahead and lock someone up.

These are all things I tried to explain to new police officers. Most listened, and a few didn't.

In 1980, the chief of police was Jack Whittinghill. He called me to his office one day and asked for a favor. The department needed someone to print photographs. There was a fully equipped darkroom at the police department, and the only officer who knew what to do in there had resigned. Jack knew I had received advanced training in photography including darkroom while with the excise police, and he asked if I would process and print the department's film. This wasn't so far back in the dark ages that we didn't have color film, but the training available for police and affordable darkroom equipment were important factors about how police handled film processing. The best thing for police was confidentiality, and that aspect was questionable then as it is today when letting outsiders see what you have taken photos of.

I agreed wholeheartedly. The chief told me that I would be called upon a few hours weekly to process film, primarily from the detectives. He explained that I wouldn't get paid, but I would earn time that I could take off later.

More than anything, I saw this as an opportunity to show my willingness to help the department and make some points toward my goal of being a detective. Up to this point, I had never officially told the department that I wished to be considered for an appointment as a detective, but I did tell Jack Whittinghill shortly after he became chief that I had a wish to be considered whenever a detective appointment opened up. Timing was everything, and I understood that with the way gossip ran through the department, that I could be undermined easily if certain people learned of my desire. I also had become an avid photographer since obtaining my photography training. Chief Whittinghill told me I could process and print my own photos in the darkroom as long as I paid for my supplies. To me, this was great.

It seemed immediate when detectives told me they had film that needed to be processed and printed. I loved the chance to do this for them and prove I kept my mouth shut about what I saw. They did some surveillances, and I thought it was great that I was in the know, and I never, ever, discussed what I saw.

It wasn't too long after I started doing this when the chief called me in to his office again. He flat out told me he was planning on appointing me as a detective sometime early in 1981. He told me that nobody knew of this except for the chief of detectives, Ron Kramer. The chief told me to keep this to myself and not to tell anyone. I asked if I could tell my wife, and he said I could, but she'd have to understand not to talk about it. He also told me I could discuss this with Ron Kramer. He told me Kramer had asked for me to be appointed. I knew one thing for sure. If I was wanted to be a detective, they would make me one. The fact I was told in April 1980 to keep this a secret was a test.

This was a point in my career I had hoped for. Keeping this secret was like being Clark Kent and want to tell just someone, anyone, that you were Superman!

As far as I knew, my wife never told anyone, and I only discussed the matter once with Ron Kramer.

I was now so motivated to perform. I worked hard on my reports and tried to be excellent in my work.

Ronald Reagan

Later that year, I felt it was because I was set to be the next detective, I was assigned what I considered a special assignment. Ronald Reagan was running for president and was making a campaign appearance in Louisville. Keeping in mind that Jeffersonville shares the Ohio River with Louisville, Jeffersonville Police would be part of the security for Mr. Reagan. Mr. Reagan would be boarding the *Belle of Louisville* paddle wheeler at a location upriver from downtown Louisville and would ride the boat down the Ohio River to the downtown area of Louisville.

Ron Kramer and other Jeffersonville detectives would be onboard the *Belle* with Louisville police and Secret Service agents. I was assigned to be in uniform, in a marked police car, and be accompanied by an agent. We would be proving security along the boat's route by following along the Indiana shore. I had never been so excited with an assignment before this came along.

I met the agent I was assigned to be with, and we went to an area along Utica Pike, across the river from where we could see the *Belle of Louisville* docked. The river is about a mile across at that point. We parked, and we waited for Mr. Reagan to board the boat and then head downstream. It seemed like it took an hour or maybe an hour and a half before things started to happen.

The agent I was with was Agent Cook. He was an Alcohol, Tobacco, and Firearms agent from Evansville, Indiana. In the short while he and I worked together, I learned a lot about him. He was planning to retire soon to Florida and had been in Louisville a day or so before we had met. The government car he drove had been called to duty at the Louisville airport where agents used it to prepare for Mr. Reagan's arrival. The plane Reagan would be arriving in would have around-the-clock security, and his car was part of it. Agent Cook had just one little problem. His personal belongings, including his change of clothing and his toothbrush, were in that car, and he had been assigned far away from the airport. He had spent the night making do without these things, and you could only imagine the frustration that would cause anyone.

Agent Cook had a portable radio to communicate with the Secret Service command post, and I, of course, had my police car radio to communicate with other officers. There really wasn't any need to talk on the radio as we all knew our assignments.

While we waited for the *Belle of Louisville* to begin its trip downstream, Agent Cook told me we would be traveling close to the river, and when we came to the point in Jeffersonville where Jeffboat was located, we would enter the plant and travel the interior roadways to keep an eye on the boat.

Jeffboat is a major shipbuilding firm and is described as the largest inland shipbuilding company in the country. It covers many acres along the riverfront, and there are cranes throughout the plant. These cranes stand very tall, and the operator can get a bird's-eye view over the entire area. Agent Cook told me there shouldn't be anyone manning the cranes as the company had been meeting with security officials about these matters.

This assignment was seemingly easier and easier the more I learned about it. There was one further thing, the bridges between Louisville and Jeffersonville would be completely closed to traffic when the *Belle of Louisville* got to a certain point close to the bridges and close to downtown Louisville. We had Jeffersonville Police officer standing by ready to close the bridges on the
Indiana side of the river once they got the word.

I only wished that I would have an opportunity to see Ronald Reagan. I'd seen him on television while growing up, and I was surprised when he was elected the governor of California. Now this actor had made it this far in getting elected as president of the United

States! I was pretty impressed with all of this now, especially considering I was part of the security team for his visit.

I knew the *Belle of Louisville* well. I had ridden on it many times. I grew up only a few blocks from the river, and I always heard the calliope on the boat when it made its excursions. That was just part of living near this river. Just as I could hear the music from the boat's calliope, I routinely always heard the banging of steel from Jeffboat. The shipyard usually ran three shifts and hearing the sounds were part of living in Jeff. Now I was part of a security detail for a presidential candidate who will be riding on the same boat I knew well, and I would need to patrol Jeffboat as the boat passed. What an honor! What an experience!

Everyone got on the *Belle*, and we watched as it left its position and headed downstream. The smoke billowed from its stacks. I was envying the Jeff detectives who were on the boat. The boat moved slowly, and I drove just as slow west along the roadway following it. When we got into Jeffboat, Agent Cook directed me at each turn. He knew where we needed to go. I had only actually driven inside the plant a couple of times before this.

While we were in the plant, the Jeff Police dispatcher radioed to one of the cars at the Indiana end of the Clark Memorial Bridge that someone had called Jeff Police to report that someone had climbed up into the framework of that bridge. We always knew that type of call to be trouble. In the past, that usually meant a suicidal person. After hearing this, Agent Cook instructed me to get to that bridge as quickly as I could. It was at that moment a whole new sense of duty kicked in. I had never felt this urgency before. I radioed to my headquarters that we were heading to the bridge, and I drove as quickly as I could with my lights and siren on. I couldn't get there quick enough.

Agent Cook then used his two-way radio to call the Secret Service command post in Louisville. I heard him repeat several times, "Cook to Command, Cook to Command," with no response. His radio had went dead. The battery was drained. I radioed my station to telephone the Secret Service command post, and our dispatcher said she didn't have the number. I told her to call Louisville Police to see if they had it. We needed to advise the officers and agents on the boat that there was a possible threat on the Clark Bridge. All of these actions were within seconds. We arrived on the bridge and blocked traffic with my police car. Traffic was heavy and hadn't yet been diverted for whatever reason. Agent Cook asked me if I had a shotgun, and when I told him I did, he told me to get it out. He said if he told me to shoot somewhere, to do it.

A Jeff Police car flew past our position into Louisville and blocked the traffic heading from Louisville on the bridge. I diligently looked through the bridge's steelwork for the person we had been told about. Agent Cook continued to try his radio and never made contact. I tried several times to radio the Jeff detectives on the *Belle*. They didn't hear me because, by this time, the boat was approaching Louisville's downtown, and the calliope I was so familiar with was playing very loud and very clear. Nobody could hear anything at this point. Agent Cook came up to me and told me he had spoken with a newspaper photographer on the sidewalk of the bridge, and he had been up in the steelwork. Agent Cook told me the news media had been warned not to do this.

Well, that apparent threat disappeared just as quick as it appeared, and here I was, standing on the bridge with my shotgun. Motorists were sitting, still watching me. They couldn't see what I saw though. I now was watching Ronald Reagan on the top level of the *Belle of Louisville* steering the boat while the music blared. It was an exciting moment in time for me. I never had seen that boat rock left and right as it did with Mr. Reagan piloting it. That was the only time I ever saw him in person.

Agent Cook asked me to drive him to the Galt House in Louisville. It was a short drive to the hotel near the river front. Mr. Reagan had already disembarked the boat and had been escorted into the same hotel. Agent Cook and I walked in right behind him, with Secret Service agents greeting us, and we found ourselves a table in the restaurant. We had a few cups of coffee while we vented our excitement. He probably reported this incident to someone. I never discussed it except to Detective Kramer. He said they couldn't hear a thing with all the noise on the boat.

Over the years, I have thought about that day. I have thought about the what-ifs many times, and I soon realized if I had needed to shoot some sniper that day, my career as a police officer would have taken a sharp turn one way or another. I wouldn't have been a *hero*, just someone who went down in some book as having done something that day. I am thankful that everything worked out, and we got to have that coffee. I hope Agent Cook has had a peaceful retirement. That was a long time ago.

I did learn that we need to have those phone numbers, and we need to keep those radios charged.

Being Respectful

I always found it very easy to just treat people nice. Unless they gave me a reason to treat them otherwise, why shouldn't I? I actually think that there are several underlying reasons why some police treat people as bad people, and we all hear about it. But I have arrested people I had been acquainted with and even friends with for such crimes as murder, robbery, burglary, and whatever. I didn't give them any break, none whatsoever, but I just treated them normal.

I was booking this one guy into the jail this Sunday evening, and I had to wait in line. There was one jailer booking prisoners in, and there were a few in front of me and this guy I was there to book. It was taking a little time, and I conversed with the other police officers who stood there with their prisoners, and I just waited my time. I will never forget the expressions on their faces when it was my turn to book my prisoner. Here I am, booking this guy I had known since high school, and all of us had been relaxed in our demeanor, and when the jailer asked me what my prisoner was being booked in on, I replied, "Murder." Even my prisoner appeared flabbergasted to hear me verbalize that. I took it in stride. Unbeknownst to all the others present, I predicted their quiet responses. During all our small talk, I actually was learning from this experience like I had learned about so many things so many times before. I have reflected on that evening many times since, and I have asked myself why I took things so calmly and let everyone around me think nothing was unusual. My answer to myself was that I wanted to show them that not everyone is evil, not everyone needs to get kicked around, and maybe some consideration of all the facts need to be looked at. I also asked myself many times what else should I have done. Should I have cleared the hallway because some desperado is coming in? No, that wasn't that at all. It was pretty simple. This guy just murdered a guy and was caught, and he and I knew it. Maybe I should have just slapped him around for a while? Nope, not going to do that. I did my job, and I did it many times just like that for a long time. I have accomplished what I have set out to do, and I have had individuals get out of prison and actually thank me for how I treated them. These same people also know I'd lock them up tomorrow if necessary.

It didn't seem too difficult for me to set the example I thought needed to be shown in order to be seen as a good officer. It didn't seem a whole lot of attention was ever paid to your job performance as long as nobody complained. I wanted the police department to see I was capable of a lot of things, and you just crossed your fingers and kept the idea in your mind that someone, somewhere, was paying attention.

It was in the fall of 1980 when the Jeffersonville Police announced to officers that a new, permanent night shift would be soon created. This new *squad* would the Crime Impact Unit. A sign-up sheet was hung on the wall for those interested in joining to sign.

This new unit would be a select group of police officers who would address the increased nighttime crimes the city was experiencing.

Burglary was up, bar fights were an every night thing, we had motorcycle gangs fighting each other, and it was seeming officers were having to fight more and more drunks during the night shift.

This new unit would wear a new type of uniform too. Tactical class B uniforms with boots and bloused trousers would be issued as well as new equipment. Night sticks were going to be made that were as big as baseball bats.

I thought this would be the most awesome experience in the world to belong to this elite unit. All of my friends, who were the younger officers, were signing up.

Every day I was being asked why I didn't sign this sheet. I wasn't much of a person to tell white lies, but I sure couldn't tell them that

I was going to be a detective soon. I was consumed with the exciting idea that I could be a detective and work with these guys and get the bad guys in jail. It was a frustrating period of time while that list hung on the wall, and I watched my buds sign up to be chosen to belong to the unit. But that frustration changed one afternoon really quickly. Chief Whittinghill had taken me aside and quietly told me he wanted me to sign up for the Crime Impact Unit. This was a shock to my whole system!

For several months I had been keeping this deep secret that I was going into detectives, and now it appeared I wasn't going to see that happen.

I signed the sheet and I was selected to belong and I tried hard to hide any disappointment and get truly excited about this new unit.

Shortly after being selected, all of the officers were told to report at a uniform store in Louisville to be fitted. The chief had me ride with him and his son-in-law who had been recently hired (and also assigned with this new unit) over to the store.

The unit began its work on the evening of November 1, 1980. We all reported to work that evening, and the TV stations were there to tell the story. One of the stations asked the chief if they could ride along with a couple of officers for the story. I was selected along with my partner, the chief's son-in-law, to be the officers who would take the TV crew out for a while. We were both interviewed and on the news for a day or so.

We did do a good job. The new unit had more energy and resources, and it was exciting.

Nobody could walk the streets at night without being checked by the police. Perhaps it was just a courtesy check to ensure their safety, or perhaps they needed to explain why they were walking between businesses that were closed at three o'clock in the morning. Forms were being filled out with these nighttime contacts with information about these individuals, and detectives were filtering through the forms as they investigated crimes.

I was just a month into enjoying this night unit when I was told by the chief I would be assigned as a detective, effective at the first of the year, January 1, 1981. My new assignment would soon be announced to the entire department, and I could now really start to enjoy this job even more!

A close second behind from wanting the best-possible home life with my family was having the best-possible law enforcement job, being a Jeffersonville Police detective.

I was on cloud nine for the rest of the year.

Being a Jeffersonville
Police Detective

I felt a little bit of jealousy within the department when I was appointed as a detective. Nobody ever congratulated me or wished me well. I merely felt like someone who had been there a short time and received a promotion. No matter how you looked at it, becoming a detective was a promotion. You had flexible schedules, you didn't take routine calls like the uniformed officers did, and the public generally respected you more. There were two ways you could deal with the antagonism you felt within the department. You could go around full-time trying to explain to fellow officers how you felt you were qualified for the appointment, or you could just go ahead and do the job and enjoy your accomplishments. That is the easy choice I made. Do what my heart desired and enjoy my career. Most all of the officers I left behind in the uniformed division either wanted to be there or had themselves wrapped up in their own little world, and they would be the ones who'd have to decide if and when to escape those worlds. I refer to the officers who seemed to enjoy the uniformed work. Some enjoyed the power, some enjoyed the respect the uniform seemed to give them, and some didn't have enough sense to do anything but live and work in a very structured environment.

I was due to begin the first Monday of January 1981. I felt set to go.

But it was the day before I was to begin when I received a telephone call at home from Lt. Rick Elliott. He was second-in-command of the detective division, and he asked me if I would meet him at the detective office that Sunday evening. I will always remember that meeting. Lieutenant Elliott wanted to meet with me to set my mind at ease. He wanted to try to explain what my new job entailed, and most of all, he didn't want me to worry about my job performance.

This meeting was the thing I needed most. As eager as I was to be a detective, I had an enormous amount of concern built up within me about whether or not I would meet the expectations of the job. I went home that Sunday evening a little past 8:30 p.m. I never felt so reassured as I felt on that drive home. Rick obviously knew what anxiety I was feeling, and he sure did a good job in alleviating it.

The first several days were just as I expected. I rode with other detectives to crime scenes and assisted. It wasn't anything I wasn't used to, but I was being trained, and I needed to pay attention to what a detective did when responding to a call. It was a little bit more than what a uniformed officer did when they were there.

When a detective arrived at any scene, they usually were in charge of that scene.

The first month or so weren't too unusual as far as the police department having any major crimes that detectives would be needed to investigate. I knew that while I was being trained, and I really liked that. I wanted to be broken in on day-to-day things, and I was hoping nothing would disrupt that.

There were only six detectives, and I felt I was the weak link. I never talked to anyone about that, but I was determined to bring myself up to speed the best I could.

After about a month on the job, I was assigned to work second shift. That normally meant working from three o'clock in the afternoon until eleven o'clock at night. Soon, I was assigned to be on-call until five o'clock each morning during the week. Plus, we all took turns being on-call from Friday evenings through Monday morning at six o'clock. When I was working Fridays, I was always working throughout the night. Technically speaking, there was some other detective assigned to be on-call after midnight Friday. I never gave any thought that perhaps someone else may have actually been on-call and able to respond to any calls early on a Saturday morning.

I was loving every moment of this job, and I never questioned any part of it. To me, I had been blessed with the dream of my life.

Some nights, I would arrive home sometime after midnight and within an hour or so, be called back out.

I never cared what I was needed for. It might have been a car wreck and someone died and photos were needed. It might have been being called to a scene where a burglar had been caught inside a business. Actually, there were some times I was called out to do things that were not necessary. There was always a lot of jealousy in the department, and there were a few times that I sat in the police station at two o'clock in the morning interviewing people for nonsense. I realized quickly that the person in charge had suggested I be called out for these sometimes *mundane* matters. When those few times arose, I also knew better than say a single word about it. If I had refused to come out, I would have had to deal with a whole lot more than the fact I had been actually called out for some unnecessary reason. My supervisors were good, and they were quick to deal with those ridiculous callouts. When I was called out, I received compensatory time, and that was more than fine with me. I enjoyed this job more than anyone ever suspected. Many times I was called out in the middle of the night just to take a few photographs. I never wanted to even suggest that a uniformed officer could have easily taken some of the photos I took if the department had provided a camera. Eventually, cameras were provided, but it always seemed someone in the uniformed division had taken the camera home with them the last time it was used, and they were on their night off. Therefore, the only camera was unavailable. That never seemed to change for the longest time.

I spent many a night with broken sleep, but that never seemed to slow me down. I took my daughters to daycare, kindergarten, and grade school in the mornings after working all night, and I didn't mind. My youth and eagerness kept me going. I felt I was the luckiest person in the world to have this dream job, a great family, and my youth was carrying me through much of it.

Working with the Exploited Child Unit

While I worked second shift with the detectives, I normally arrived at two o'clock, and sometimes they would let me change the time to three o'clock. There were always so many things going on that adjusting my schedule was necessary in order for me to do the things I needed to do.

If I was assigned to interview someone who didn't get off work themselves until late in the evening, then I needed to work late as well.

There was one day when I showed up for work that I will always remember. I arrived at the office, and there were several detectives there including the chief of detectives, Ron Kramer.

Captain Kramer was always polite when he would assign me a task, and this day wasn't any different from the many days I worked for him. I hadn't been at the office, but for a few minutes when Captain Kramer said, "Flee, I was wondering if you'd do me a favor this evening." He always called me Flee, and he always asked for a *favor*. Whatever the favor was that he needed, he knew he'd get it from me.

Captain Kramer told me that there was a group of police officers who had called him from Louisville and had asked for assistance that evening. Captain Kramer told me that he didn't know too much about what they needed, but I needed to meet them at seven o'clock at the Waffle and Steak. He told me that there were a couple of social workers who'd be there, as well as police officers.

I was intrigued. I was also confused why I would be meeting social workers. I was also curious as to what they needed from the Jeffersonville Police.

Captain Kramer may or may not have known exactly what I was getting into, but I will never forget that meeting.

I arrived at the Waffle and Steak exactly at seven o'clock that evening. There were four men who I met there, and one was a Louisville Police Department detective assigned to that department's youth bureau. The others were social workers.

These people quickly explained to me that they represented the Louisville and Jefferson County Exploited Child Unit. I instantly recognized who these people were. I had seen them on the television news just the night before. I wasn't exactly sure what an exploited child was, but I had a pretty good idea. I had already been involved with some child molestation investigations, and even though the word *exploited* never came up, I figured it was pretty close to what this was all about.

The news I had seen the evening before was about this Exploited Child Unit arresting a minister in Louisville for having sex with young boys.

In a nutshell, I was quickly educated to a phenomenon that was occurring in Louisville and, from the Exploited Child Unit's knowledge, had only been seen recently before in Chicago. This was early 1981, and I couldn't imagine how something like this had been going on, especially for any length of time. But what I learned was shocking, and I knew I was about to delve head first into an investigation involving this phenomenon.

What was happening was this: young males in Louisville were frequenting this particular city park in an area near the Louisville downtown. These young boys, mostly within the ages of twelve and fifteen, were making themselves available to grown men. The term *pedophile* was around back then, but there were other terms used for men who would prey on young boys for sex. Perverts was at the top of the list, and child molester was a close second. The term *pedophile* was soon to become a term that would be readily assigned to certain individuals. I would also be finding myself very close to a social turn our world would be making in an awakening of the victimization of our children. I was seated on the front row of this awakening, but it took me a little time to realize the experience would play out to be.

I met with these members of the Exploited Child Unit long enough to realize a couple of things. First, they had been involved in investigations that had been quite confidential and, until the news broke the previous evening, not too many people knew much about the Exploited Child Unit nor about the scope of the problem. I felt I was totally on top of police operations in the Louisville and Southern Indiana area, and it was surprising to me to find I wasn't there at all.

The meeting with the unit was to the point. They had been instrumental in bringing down criminal charges on this minister, and their investigation had led them to Indiana. A large percentage of the boys they had been interviewing in that case had also told investigators about this man from Southern Indiana who they also knew. It seemed this man would drive by this city park when he got off from work and *cruise* looking for a young boy to take home with him. They wanted to bust him right away. The following night was agreed upon, and things went great after we had set a date.

I received a quick rundown of what was happening from the director of the Exploited Child Unit. The director, John Rabun, told me that what they had found was that these kids that were being victimized weren't necessarily runaways, but kids who had a poor lifestyle. These were boys who probably had a home, with a single parent, normally a mother, and maybe a sibling or two. They usually didn't live too far from this park, were all well acquainted, and knew the situation quite well.

These boys would make themselves available in the evenings at the park, awaiting to be approached by one of these men who were looking for sex with a boy. These boys were not necessarily homosexual but did, for the most part, receive some oral sexual gratification from the men they went with. More than anything though, the men showered these boys with a good meal, a nice place to relax, perhaps drugs and alcohol, and maybe even some pornography. In the case in Southern Indiana, this was what was going on and more. The boys who had been interviewed so far had also told about trips to the Cincinnati Reds games and trips to Florida. It was explained to me that the boys came from poor families, and their parent(s) didn't know much more that this guy was nice and a friend of so-and-so and wanted to take a group of the boys to a game or to Florida. This was quite a great experience and treat for these kids in the eyes of these normally single parents and was quite welcomed. It was something they otherwise would not be able to experience. The part about sex was not in the line of information being fed to the adult. I also learned that these men knew the program and played into it well. This was the phenomenon.

I learned from the Exploited Child Unit that the guy they were now focusing on was named Jack, and he worked not far from the park where these boys hung out. This Jack was known to drive a Cadillac and would routinely drive by the park when he got off from work at eleven o'clock in the evening. All that the boys had told investigators was that he would pick one of them up and drive to his apartment in Indiana. Sex would take place involving whatever boy was with Jack, and the boy would be returned to the park a while afterward. These kids didn't know the name of the city where he lived, but they knew it wasn't far after they crossed the bridge.

The city of Louisville is right along the Ohio River, and the river is the state line when you look where the line is between Indiana and Kentucky. There were two bridges, and either is about a mile long. The two Indiana municipalities directly across the river at the bridges are Clarksville and Jeffersonville. This made up much of the metropolitan area. It was decided that a Clarksville Police officer should be involved in the event this Jack guy lives in Clarksville, and I assured the investigators I would take care of being sure that Clarksville Police would be involved. All of us knew we would need to keep in mind that Indiana and Kentucky have two separate set of criminal laws. Working as a police officer in the area, we knew we always needed to keep this in mind. This wasn't always easy, but something that was always done.

Aside from being an important "child molester" case, working across state lines was not something we were unaccustomed to. We knew our area and what we needed to deal with. I could only imagine what it would be like working near Canada or Mexico and working with those laws and jurisdictions.

The following day, I telephoned Captain Kramer and explained to him what I was working on. He assured me he would see that Clarksville Police would be contacted to see if they wanted to send someone to assist. When I arrived to work that next afternoon, he told me that Clarksville Detective Gary Hall would be getting with me, and we could work together.

The plan was that I, and whomever Clarksville sent, would meet a member of the Exploited Child Unit about nine thirty and get a portable radio in order to communicate with the Exploited Child Unit investigators. Detective Hall and I got together, and we met with the unit member and retrieved our radio. This was a radio working on the Louisville Police frequency, and we were advised to monitor the surveillance when Jack got off from work.

Things worked a lot different back then. We didn't have cell phones, and if you did want to chat by a telephone, you better have a coin for a payphone and know a number where the other person would be sure to answer. But we didn't have cell phones because they didn't exist. But what we did have was a plan. We had our plan together and details worked out. We just needed to listen to this police radio and respond accordingly. Neither Detective Hall nor I knew what to expect this evening as this type of surveillance was new to us both, and it was anyone's guess where the case would land, Jeffersonville or Clarksville. Gary told me he hadn't heard about this Exploited Child Unit either before the news broke earlier in the week.

We knew that Jack would be getting off from work at eleven o'clock that evening, and it went like clockwork. We overheard detectives talking about watching him leave work in his car and drive toward the park.

It wasn't a moment or two until we overheard the officers report that Jack had picked up a young boy who appeared to be under fifteen years of age and were driving toward Indiana. Gary Hall and I quipped about whose jurisdiction this would all land in, but when we overheard that Jack had taken the Jeffersonville exit, we both knew whose lap this was all headed toward. Actually, I was very excited, intrigued, fascinated, eager to see what would happen next, and most of all, wondering what I would need to do next.

This was quickly becoming a moment of reckoning for me. I had been involved in several police operations up to this point, and I have made some command moves. This was landing right in my lap, and I knew I had better have a plan.

I had never been involved in anything quite like this before, and I sure didn't know anyone who had. I was accepting this challenge and ready to do whatever I had to do.

Detective Hall and I had overheard the other officers give out the Cadillac's license plate number, and I had our dispatcher run it to see who it came back to. The address we received was at a Jeffersonville apartment complex, and we headed there. Detective Hall and I parked right outside the address given and waited. The Louisville Police radio was working fine, but the Louisville Police radio repeaters were not set up to pick up low-powered two-way radios from Indiana. Therefore, what we were hearing was breaking up badly. We did hear enough to know that Jack in his Cadillac and this teenaged boy were pulling into the entrance of the apartment complex. I watched the car pull in, and then behind it, I saw about six or seven other nondescript cars. I felt those must be surveillance units. They seemed to magically disappear once entering the complex.

Detective Hall and I watched from just a matter of feet the Cadillac. It parked right in front of us, and this man and boy exited and walked right into the apartment, and I reported on the license plate registration. No violation of any Indiana state law had yet been witnessed. My mind was on full speed while watching the unfolding event, and I hadn't seen anything wrong yet. I was already clear that the Kentucky officers had observed a misdemeanor violation of their state laws, but I was keeping a clear view on my end of the stick. They had a law about an unlawful transaction with a minor that they could apply, but things weren't the same in Indiana. I would be required to actually see with my own eyes some things, and that especially applied toward misdemeanors. That was as far as dealing with an adult. I knew the teenager was at risk, but I needed just a little bit more to not only protect him but also at the same time convict Jack.

That is where my mind was focused. I knew I had very little time. I really knew that when Jack and the boy had entered the apartment building out of our view. This really came into mind when I was quickly approached by several Kentucky officers who looked at me and asked, "What are you going to do?" This is a feeling and moment all police officers should experience. It should be mandatory. You have to make a decision and make it right now. I made one.

Here I was, the big detective I wanted to become. Now, I had been placed into a situation where I was needed to prove I could do the right thing. I was dealing with something that had been handed to me dealing with the laws of Kentucky and Indiana. I was also dealing with the urgency of a child at risk. That part was foremost in my mind. But I needed to act in such a way as not to jeopardize the criminal case I had in mind.

I didn't need much time to think about the decision I had made. I told the other officers, "I'm going to knock on the door." I didn't have the time to explain what or why I was doing this, but I remember all so well the others whispering to each other, "Yeah."

I entered the apartment building quietly. I knew the layout very well. My parents had lived next door just a few years earlier while trying to reconcile, and I had lived in the complex a year after getting married. I knew where I was at.

I walked quietly to the door where Jack supposedly lived. I had only seen him enter the outer door but felt certain he was where he was listed as living. The other detectives were just as quiet as they stepped just inside the outer door and watched me.

I went to the door where Jack supposedly lived, and I knocked a couple of times. I intently looked through the glass peephole for any movement within the apartment and saw none. However, immediately after knocking on the door, I heard a man answer. The man sounded as if he was very close to the door. I hadn't seen any movement, and it didn't seem as if someone approached the door after I had knocked. The man answered, "Who is it?"

I responded, "Sir, I think I may have backed into your car, and I wanted you to take a look at it." I just wanted that door opened.

The man responded, "Who are you?" And I responded, "My name is Jack, and I think I just hit your car."

The man inside answered back very politely, "Sir, I don't know anyone named Jack. Are you sure you have the right apartment?" It didn't take but a microsecond for me to respond in a very not polite voice, "This is Detective Jack Fleeman of the Jeffersonville Police Department, and I need you to open your door now!"

The door couldn't have opened any quicker. I think it was with the urgency and demand and how I verbalized it, but he opened right then. Jack stood at the door and within a couple of feet from the door was a white male, age fourteen, sitting on an overstuffed chair, pulling his trouser zipper up. The chair was so close to the front door that I understood why I hadn't seen movement through the peephole.

I was in charge now. I didn't need to think any more about it. I had all the information I needed to tell this man to have a seat, and about eight of us entered his apartment.

Jack was not his real name, but a name he went by. He worked as a photographer at a Louisville lithograph company. The young teen told us all about how Jack had been performing oral sex on him when I had knocked on the door.

We received consent to search the apartment. Dozens of photographs of victims of the Louisville minister were found. They were found to be this guy's victims just as well. We found pornography and photos of this guy with kids at the Cincinnati Reds games and in Florida.

Jack sat down on the living room couch while we searched his apartment. One of us was always watching him while the others searched. The investigators from Louisville kept commenting about what they were seeing, and I had to ask what they were seeing. It was learned that all of the boys who had been the victim of the Louisville minister and had told them about also being involved with Jack had given very detailed descriptions of Jack's apartment, including swords hanging near a mirror in the living room.

I was quickly learning something about investigations. We were tying in one perpetrator to several victims of another *perp*. That is the term I soon learned about these perverts who victimized people for their sexual desires.

I had never yet been involved in such a search. I had served search warrants for stolen property and drugs and booze, but this was quite different. Here I was, in charge of a search being performed by the Jeffersonville Police and aside from Gary Hall from Clarksville being there, I was on my own. These guys from Kentucky were just that, guys from another state, where laws differ.

I felt a little bit apprehensive but still confident during the search. There was one thing that happened though that eased my mind—that I was doing the right thing. While Jack was seated in the front room, he had asked someone if he could use the bathroom. Of course, we all agreed, since he was allowing us to search his home. I was in his bedroom searching his dresser drawers while he was in the bathroom, and it was then I heard the most unusual noise. Having once lived in the apartment complex, I knew what I heard. There were ceiling lights in the bathroom, and semitransparent light lenses were installed instead of dropped ceiling tiles, and they made a familiar sound when they were moved.

While Jack was in the bathroom and we heard that sound, I immediately told the others what we were hearing. We had already searched him and pretty well searched his bathroom before giving him a moment in there alone, but I knew what I heard. We opened the bathroom door and saw Jack actually trying to stick metal movie film reels down his toilet. We grabbed the reels, and we led him back into his living room to sit back down on his couch. Of course he didn't flush any movie reels, but we knew he tried to destroy evidence. A quick scan of the filmstrips showed us he was trying to destroy pornographic movies. The Louisville investigators then told me that the boys from the minister case had told them Jack sometimes showed porn in order to arouse them for sex.

We removed bags of evidence from that apartment that evening. We searched for over two hours, and we felt we had found everything. We didn't arrest Jack that evening. I had been instructed to be cautious about any warrantless arrest, plus I still wanted his *cooperative spirit* to live on until he showed up the next afternoon in order for me to get a tape-recorded statement from him.

Jack ended up being arrested. His name was in the paper, and he agreed to go to prison for an eight-year term.

I had learned he had molested other boys in Jeffersonville a few years before I charged him. He had been charged in those cases but never sentenced to prison. I met with the judge on those charges one afternoon, and he explained a few things to me that I already understood. Jack was a perpetrator, and our city, town, county, society, or whatever, did not want to admit these problems existed. These were things families dealt with within, and nobody wanted the embarrassment of being known as a victim of such private things. He had told Jack to get counseling and to stay away from young boys. He said that this is what the community expected, and no more. I understood that. I didn't agree, but I understood where things were at. The judge told me that those boys would have been ruined in the community if what had happened was publicized.

I knew at that very time things needed to change. There was absolutely no way a man could routinely perform oral sex on young boys for his own sexual gratification and just be ignored. Even if these boys knew what they were subjecting themselves to. Especially if I considered this perp's next victim wasn't a kid waiting in a park to have sex with some old man in order for this kid to go to Disney World or a ballgame.

These boys that Jack had victimized told me all about how a group of them traveled to Florida for this fun trip that their single moms welcomed as a treat for their boys from this nice man. The photos Jack had saved in his dresser showed them posing at the Florida State Line sign. I always remember those photos when I see that state line sign. It doesn't matter if it was that same sign, or one a hundred miles away, I remember it.

The interviews with the young boys seemed identical. They all went to Florida, checked in to this motel with Jack, and knew what to expect. They were going to be treated royally on this trip, but there was a fee. They all told me about how while at the motel pool, they went one by one up to the motel room alone to be with Jack.

It was there that the boys told me that they allowed Jack to perform oral sex on them. That was what they did for this trip. They told me how they would speak individually and privately amongst each other about what was going on all while swimming in the pool. One by one, each would take his turn to visit the motel room to be alone with Jack.

These boys all went home with experiences, other than sex with Jack, that most all kids would enjoy. If it had not been for Jack, or some other *perp*, perhaps these boys would never see Florida, Disney World, or a Cincinnati Reds game.

If nothing else, they got a ride out of the city, maybe smoked a little pot. Some said they sometimes received sexual gratification, but for the most part, they got a break and were treated nice. They got more than if they had stayed home and lived in not necessarily horrible conditions, but they had a good ride.

This was the phenomenon that was happening in our community, country, and probably plenty of more places. We had to grab this thing and do more than get a handle on it.

It seemed like every other day that I would get a phone call from John Rabun telling me that another victim of Jack had been located. John always made the necessary arrangements for me to arrive at his office, and this new kid be there for me to interview. I always will remember how these young boys wanted me to remember that they were not gay by any means.

I ended up with a total of twenty-five young boy victims in this investigation.

When I went to one of these kid's home to bring him in for his statement, he had married, and he made sure that when I arrived to pick him up, his wife knew I was a probation officer. He surely didn't want her to know what he had been involved in, and he especially didn't want her to think he was gay.

I had seen enough. I routinely spoke with Ron Kramer about what I had seen, and he was very receptive to everything I had learned about this case.

Another detective with the Jeff Police was Ray Leezer. Ray and I had worked some with the Jefferson County, Kentucky Police

Department. Louisville is in Jefferson County in Kentucky and at the time, there was the Louisville Police Department that was within the actual city limits of Louisville, and there was the Jefferson County Police which handled policing the areas outside Louisville's city limits. There were a few smaller city departments within Jefferson County as well. Shively, Jeffersontown, and St. Matthews all had their own police departments as well. Jefferson County police was a big department and was an excellent department, just like Louisville Police. Jefferson County Police Department's Criminal Intelligence Division had a couple of detectives who knew Ray and knew the work I had done with the Jefferson County Exploited Child Unit. We assisted them with an undercover investigation also going on in the Louisville area. A person, possibly representing an organization of people, was recruiting young boys for a pornographic operation. The main guy, a white man, middle-aged, usually accompanied by a couple of similarly described men were hanging out at this Louisville restaurant and recruiting boys.

I cannot tell you how many hours of surveillance, pots of coffee I must have drank, and pieces of pie I know I ate while doing my part of this surveillance. I never enjoyed sitting out in the van just watching, but you can only sit in a restaurant and eat so much pie and drink so much coffee. It reminded me of sitting in bars while working for the excise police. That was a little more relaxing, but not near as important of the type of work I was now doing.

It was unbelievable how many young boys approached the men in the restaurant and knew to ask for *work*. I never knew the total outcome of the investigation as I just did the part I was asked to do. I did learn from these other detectives that there was a thriving sex industry amongst us all, and we were just tapping into a little corner of it.

It wasn't until a short time later that a member of the Exploited Child Unit asked for me to help on another investigation. It seemed a ranking member of the Louisville Police had a daughter who had been a runaway from her home for some time and had recently been returned home. The Exploited Child Unit had been called in because the girl had told her father a few things we all needed to know.

It seemed that while this high school–aged girl had been on the run, she got involved with some people who gave her a place to live. This was a house just outside the Jeffersonville city limits. While staying there, the girl was made to perform in pornographic movies being made at the house. This supposedly went on for a couple of weeks. The girl had told investigators that the men who made the films had been placing the recorded tapes in a basket on a hallway floor at the end of each evening's filming. The tapes were always gone by the time this girl woke the following morning. This girl also told investigators that the house was painted purple and had no telephone. She told them that there were a few other young people staying at this house who sometimes went with her to the closest payphone.

You have to keep in mind, this is the early 1980s. Cell phones were nonexistent, and if you needed to make a telephone call, you needed a telephone landline. This girl said that purple house didn't have a phone, but a couple of young people who had been staying there led her across a couple of fields to a truck stop near I-65 where payphones were at. It was almost a mile walk.

The investigator from the Exploited Child Unit and I looked for a few hours for this house, but we never found it. Later that day, a narcotics detective I worked with, Donnie Croft, told me he knew the house well. He showed me the house that evening. I had been so close but had not driven down this one road far enough. I saw it though, that purple house. It was now abandoned. Detective Croft had served a search warrant there not that long ago, but he seized drugs. It didn't surprise him that child porn was being made there, but he told me he hadn't seen evidence of porn when he was there.

About this same time, Detective Leezer received information from Houston, Texas. Police in that area were investigating the murder of a young boy who had been found to have been involved in child porn. Telephone records in their investigation led to them to a pay phone at the same truck stop near the purple house. I never learned whatever came out of that. I never forgot it either.

As time went on, Detective Leezer and I worked routinely with the Exploited Child Unit. We both were asked to assist them this one Friday evening to check porn stores. They had assembled several teams of about five officers each to check each and every adult store in Jefferson County, Kentucky. If I remember right, there were probably about a dozen. A few were downtown in Louisville, and some were out in the county near strip joints. Each team was assigned to check each location. We were looking for any evidence of children being exploited. That meant checking magazines, and I mean thoroughly, visiting the peep shows, visually checking employees, and looking at the movie racks. I somehow always felt the store employees knew who we were, even though we tried to look like a group of guys on a bachelor party, or you can guess what we may or may not have looked to be. I always remember one thing though. Whenever I exited one of those places, I always felt that Pastor Vogler from Faith Lutheran Church was sitting at the stoplight and watching me exit with the group. Pastor Vogler was the minister of the church I attended then. I was so relieved when I told him this story and my concerns. He assured me he never saw me, so I didn't need to be concerned. He is a great guy. I just wish he hadn't smirked the way he did when I gave him my *confession*. Ah, what the heck, he knows I am doing my job.

One day soon after these events, Detective Leezer and I received an invitation. The Louisville and Jefferson County Exploited Child Unit were hosting the International Symposium for Exploited Children. This convention was to be of a group of people just like us. Any person involved in child victimization were invited. It was held at the Hyatt Regency Hotel in downtown Louisville.

The symposium ended up being a three-day event that I could never forget, and it was something that influenced me forever.

Having been a police officer and just living in our world, I knew that horrible things were happening to our children and not a whole lot being done about a lot of it. There was a whole bunch of concerns, a whole bunch of "if I onlys", and a whole lot more of "something needs to be dones" going around in any circles you were in. This included at home, at work, at church, at the police department, or while with friends.

Everyone could turn on the television or pick up a newspaper and read about some horrible crimes against children.

I still remember the surprise I felt when I had seen on television that this Exploited Child Unit not only existed but caught this minister using young boys. That meant someone had done something. And a couple of days later, I had done the same thing. What was happening?

Change was going on.

I was keen to what our local area tolerated, and when something was dealt with, it was understood. I tried to keep in mind what that judge had tried to explain to me. I was motivated to some degree to focus on these issues, but I was a general purpose police detective. I would soon learn to tailor my thinking and efforts to the goals that needed to be met and still focus on other duties. After all, someone's business might be burglarized tomorrow night, and I'd be called on to deal with it.

This was what I wanted. I probably was the luckiest police officer in the world. I saw Louisville detectives work solely on select type of crimes, but I got it all. I was able to incorporate my ideas into new developing strategies toward investigations and steer them toward the goal of making our community a little bit safer, and hopefully setting the stage for future law enforcement to have some guidelines to follow. One of the first things I knew when I came to the Jeffersonville Police Department was the department needed guidance and stability. I would later learn that the guidance would come at a slow pace, and the stability was never a certain thing. Politics played so much of a part in everyday police activities, and if someone in authority didn't want something a certain way, it wouldn't. At least while they were in power, so wait a few years and perhaps the next election would allow for a few things to get better. The younger officers was where it has always been at. Educate them, make them see what needs to be done for the right reasons, educate them about the politics, and cross your fingers. The person you might hope would be the best person to change things might give up, align themselves with a politician, and set themselves up for a day when they would become ineffective, or perhaps someday be recognized as a true leader and get something accomplished.

I can say that with changes in politics, I never saw anything go backward as far as progress is concerned. I have seen complete dormant times, however, when someone got the reins on the department and stood absolutely still during their tenure.

I never claimed to be the perfect person for any job at the police department. What I did do, however, was see what needed to be done to aim the department toward being better. The department had a whole lot of awakening to do, and I felt fortunate to be where I was at the time I was there. It was a time of change. I just hoped I could contribute some guidance and be part of the positive changes. I also wanted to enjoy a career as a Jeffersonville Police Officer. I was doing that. Any new officer that came to the department, and I had some time to influence them, I took advantage of that time and tried to make them see where the department had been, where it was presently at, and where it needed to go. No one person would be able to do those tasks.

Politics was and still is the biggest obstacle for the department.

This symposium may have influenced me more than most, but here is what it was.

Experts from not only Louisville but also from all over the United States talked about the victimization of children that was going on in our world and how people had a tendency to ignore it. The attention focused on this reason of ignoring the problem and how it was causing long-term effects on the victims.

The symposium also focused on how there were no known cures or treatment for these *perps*, and that the courts needed to realize this and deal with it.

The event brought attention to the fact that the family unit was a factor in protecting *Uncle Fred* for what he had done to little *Johnny*, and this needed to change.

Child murder was a major portion of this conference. I had known about several cases, and the parents of these children appeared on a panel one morning of the symposium.

One of the cases presented was about Etan Patz, age six. He had went to the bus stop in New York one morning in the late 1970s and never boarded the bus. The teachers never told the school office that he was absent, and it wasn't until after he didn't get off the school bus shortly after three o'clock that afternoon that authorities were notified. Etan's mother told her story that morning in Louisville that left the entire assembly dead silent.

Amongst several other parents who had their own nightmares to tell, John and Reve Walsh told us about their son Adam.

They had been at a mall in Florida and had lost sight of Adam for a few moments while in a store. They never saw him again.

John Walsh told the audience about when a few weeks earlier, he and his wife had appeared as a guest with David Hartman on ABC's *Good Morning America*. I will always remember his recollection of a phone call he received moments before he and his wife were due to go on TV. He told us that police in Florida had just recovered his son's head, and then he had to go on national television a few moments after the call. As I sat in the audience, I wondered how many others had seen him that morning. I did. As I remember that, he explained how difficult it was to go ahead with the television show appearance.

We had representatives from the United States Postal Service tell us about how the postal inspectors worked on the child exploitation issues that used the mail service. They explained they dealt with groups that, to some degree, were protected under our constitution who had a routine mailing list. They told us about one such group whose motto was "sex before eight before it's too late."

I experienced quite a bit of *shock therapy* with that symposium. I was more than impressed with the entire program. I was more impressed with those who set the whole program up.

I had found myself experiencing this whole program with a whole lot of people just like me.

The final day of this symposium involved the participants talking amongst themselves.

I found myself sitting in discussion groups with police officers, child welfare workers, medical people, social workers, teachers, and others who had been dealing with these problems in their home states and countries.

The one thing we all left that conference with was a single issue. We all agreed to return to our home areas and spread the word. We needed to tell the world that these violations against our children are wrong, and it is just as wrong not to address it in such a way that the perps go unpunished.

We all agreed that just getting family members to protest and testify against one another would be a major undertaking in the society in which we were living.

We left that event with those thoughts and commitments. I had never been so impressed with what I had just experienced in my law enforcement career.

This was like no other training gathering I had ever attended. I found myself amongst of people just like me, including a woman from Belgium, promising one another that we would return to our communities and *spread the word*. That we would try to educate those around us of how we need to change our way of thinking. I readily agreed, and I left that symposium with a whole bunch of eagerness and concern that this might not be readily accepted.

When I returned to work, I explained to all of my fellow detectives and sometimes the chief of what I had learned. Usually when you would return from a school, you would find yourself keeping your newfound knowledge to yourself. This was because the more experienced officers already knew what you had learned. They probably went to the same school sometime earlier. But this seemed different. Most of us had worked child molesting cases, and we all knew the obstacles an investigator was likely to encounter during any given investigation. I had some suggestions that I brought back, and I certainly did not receive any obstacles when I suggested ways of following through with the suggested ideas.

You see, I was normally assigned to second shift. I suggested that I carry some of the ideas, thoughts, experiences of others, or whatever I could deliver, to PTA groups. These groups later became known as PTO. Parent Teacher Association or Parent Teacher Organization, whatever they called themselves, I wanted to be a guest speaker for their meetings.

That idea sure didn't take long to take off. The police department was always near the top of the lists of these organizations to call on for a program. Now, instead of sending someone to talk about self-defense, burglary prevention, or driver improvement, I made myself available to talk to groups about child molestation.

I began speaking every month to PTO or PTA groups. I began to feel so comfortable telling groups of adults about the crimes I knew about, the secrecy that was embedded within families, and the lack of prosecution due to these secrets that were withheld. It was so awesomely surprising to me about how well received I was giving these talks.

I had prepared myself to get a backlash from a few, an argument here and there, and an eventual reduction in the invitation to these meetings. That did not happen at all. The opposite happened. I found the attendance grew at the school meetings once they found out the guest speaker would be talking about molestation and that children perhaps shouldn't be attending.

One night at Northaven Elementary School, I was honored to present a couple of members from the Louisville Exploited Child Unit to speak. That night, parents received the *full boat* of information. I was so totally excited about what I was involved in. That evening, John Rabun, the director of the Exploited Child Unit, along with Kerry Rice, a member of the unit, spoke about how the family unit needed to get together and understand that these *family secrets* about *Uncle so and so* or whoever, had to be stopped from molesting any more children. Family members were being taught the problem, the results of the problems, and most of all, to take a step outside the family and get outside help. Embarrassment wasn't an excuse anymore. That was the message we were delivering.

One night I tried to speak at such a meeting, and I had so much disruption as parents kept pointing and trying to direct my attention to this man sitting amongst them. I knew what they were trying to signal me, but I will never, ever, forget how welcome they made me feel and asked for my help. I was seeing a little effort on my part, as well as others, taking tremendous strides. It became quite apparent that people were just looking for an excuse, a reason, a change in attitude, or perhaps a bit of knowledge that there were others outside their family unit that might just know what they were going through, and not only understood it but also were waiting to deal with it on their family's behalf. They knew it was well understood that it was a major gamble in a family's relationship within their unit, for one to have the courage to step outside that unit and file a police report.

It started to happen. It started to increase so much that all of the officers were commenting how we received more child molesting reports from family members. We all knew it was a very good thing, and the support from the judicial side seemed to follow just as well as the law enforcement side. The judges and prosecutors attended some of the training I had, and I knew they were also being trained within their professional circles. Things were changing. I am just referring to my local area where I lived and worked. That was the area I served and could only affect. But I read and heard stories about the same things going on everywhere. I didn't have any reason to think I hadn't had some influence on a few things. I felt great. This is what I wanted to do in my career. Do a good job, and maybe make some things better.

One of the biggest honors I received was an annual invitation from Providence High School to speak with a class of senior girls who were ready to graduate after taking a family-oriented course preparing them for life as a parent.

The letters I received from those girls far outweighed any commendation the police department might have given me. I have always known I might have given a few of those students some good tools to use when dealing with some of life's complications. Plus, they may remember a cop gave them those tools. I did this for about three years. I loved it.

During this same time, I was invited to become a member of a special task force sponsored by Jefferson County, Kentucky Government. Then county judge Mitch McConnell created this task force to address problems within our world involving child victimization. I had already met John Walsh at the symposium, and I found him to be a regular attendee and speaker at the task force meetings. It was at one meeting that he made a point about police that I was able to take back to the Jeffersonville Police and see a change of policy within the same week.

I had taken it upon myself to read about things involving crimes against children, and the tragedy of Adam Walsh was always mentioned. Not to single this tragedy out from others, but John Walsh had the tools, forethought, emotion, reason, energy, desire, and whatever other drives he certainly felt, and I was always reading and hearing his name. I read some articles that suggested his efforts were self-serving. And I also wondered about that. I had read somewhere that Mr. Walsh was in the midst of a marketing or public relations career when his son was murdered, and writers said he might be publicizing on the tragedy to further his career. I have always kept those comments in mind and watched how things developed over many years. The entire world should be thankful of how he saw what had happened to his son, how he tried to let the law enforcement system give him the answers he and his wife needed to hear and see. He gave his trust to the *system* to lead him through the ordeal.

The system needs to fully understand how he changed things.

I recall clearly the comments he made at one of those task force meetings. He told the group, there were probably forty or fifty of us attending, about an absolute true fact that I quickly became ashamed of. John Walsh told the group that law enforcement needed to change. He stated that if he had to report his car stolen, the police would immediately take the report, and within a very short time, the car would be entered into the National Crime Information Computer (NCIC) for the whole country to be on the lookout. He also stated that if he were to make a similar call that his young son was missing, he would be told that a report would not be taken for twenty-four hours. John Walsh must have been speaking to me. He was right. The Jeffersonville Police Department did have that exact policy. From what I knew, all police had that policy. Kids ran away all the time. It was a big effort to enter anything into NCIC. I always have understood what the reason was for this, and it is hard to explain. Basically, it all led to the quality of people working as police officers.

Not at all to criticize them, but you need to understand the way our world was developing and how society thought about some things. I already knew I was in the midst of a whole lot of changes about how police operated, and I felt it as a challenge to be there.

I met with my chief of police the very next day along with my chief of detectives. I had asked for the meeting. I simply explained what John Walsh had presented, and within a fifteen-minute meeting, I was assured things would change. With a simple directive, the following day, Chief Whittinghill changed the department's policy when taking missing person's reports. Reports would be taken immediately, and information entered into NCIC. It was a done deal. I wonder how long it would have otherwise taken to get that policy changed. I started to see other departments quickly change their policy as well. This was another change I was able to witness.

John Walsh was instrumental in the establishment of the National Center of Exploited and Missing Children. Many of the Louisville unit went on to work there as active employees or board members. When that happened, I realized how fortunate I was to have worked with them.

It wasn't a long time later until I was able to attend a three-day school in Chicago about homicide training. The chief of detectives Ron Kramer took me and another detective to the school. The training came from investigators just like us who had been involved in some very trying cases, and they offered many valuable suggestions. We heard from FBI profilers, as well as detectives from departments who had worked on the Green River killings and also the John Wayne Gacy killings.

The three of us talked quite a bit on the drive home about what we had learned. We agreed that one policy our department had was also needing to be addressed. The detectives who had investigated the Gacy killings had told us that perhaps police would have gotten a handle on the problem earlier if they had done something different. Those detectives told us about a policy they had concerning reports on missing children. Keeping in mind that most in the training seemed to have gotten on board with the new idea of taking missing children reports right away, theirs was another suggestion.

Those detectives told us of the clues they might have grasped, the evidence they might have obtained, the observations they might have made, and maybe even the knowledge that something horrible was happening if their departments had done one thing differently. Their police departments, just like the Jeffersonville Police Department, had a policy that people wanting to make a missing person report had to come to police headquarters to file the report. This included missing children. We had learned that if officers had actually went into the homes of these missing children that Gacy had killed, they might have seen something, a clue, found anything, while taking the missing person report, to raise a red flag. During that drive home, Ron Kramer said he would meet with Chief Whittinghill as soon as we got back to suggest a change.

I realized he must have had that meeting with the chief the very next evening I was working. This is because I was out on an investigation when the radio dispatcher called me on the police radio and dispatched me to take a missing juvenile report. I clearly recall the feeling that ran through me. This type of call was always assigned to a uniformed officer, and the dispatcher was giving it to me. I already had the tools within me to understand what was happening. The uniformed division was feeling that a couple of detectives had went to a school and came back with added work for an already busy uniformed division. It was a signal to me that if you want this done this way, you go do it. Within a short time after being told to take this report, a uniformed officer radioed in that he's going to take the call. The officers who were working and heard the radio traffic all got the underlying message. I spent a few days trying to explain why the new rule was put into place, and they seemed to understand. Things were changed then and remained that way today.

I attended one other school later that taught me about myself. This training made me realize that police officers are reluctant to change. I couldn't agree more. I attribute that to the fact that police are required to so many things, perform so many duties, leave such a great impression with everyone they deal with, and work under-staffed almost all the time. Police need a little more push to take on even more duty. Police do hesitate to change, but even though they might be a little behind the times, they do always fall into the game. Some departments are quicker to adapt to some things than others. You need to keep in mind that police departments work for their community, and politics, pay levels, workloads, and local values always seem to influence how things run.

I will always remember a day when a fellow detective took a call from a police department from a large West Coast city. The department was needing some help from us, and the Jeff detective asked the person to whom he was speaking to try to understand that "we were just getting out of leisure suits here in Jeffersonville." We always have been a little behind the times. Since the detective was actually speaking with another policeman, the exaggeration was well understood. My leisure suit had been gone for years! However, my department was like many others, and change was slow. Other longtime officers will understand what I mean.

Working as a detective was always exciting, tiring, informative, an honor, and more than anything else, what I lived to do. I was blessed to have the opportunity to live the job that I had dreamed of. I wasn't by any means the best. I never have thought that. But I tried my best. I met many detectives from many departments, and they weren't any different than me. I always knew I was fortunate to work for the Jeffersonville Police. This was the department that was growing out of a small city and into a bigger and better department. I knew I wasn't cut out to be the chief or any position that would take me away from investigations, but I wanted to have a little influence when it came to thinking *outside the bun*. Being a small department right next to a city the size of Louisville offered many opportunities that other similarly sized departments would not necessarily experience. This means the good, the bad, and everything in between.

There have been dozens of cases I was involved in aside from dealing with the never-ending child molesting cases I have worked.

Murder, burglary, theft, assault, along with a slew of other criminal charges have been filed after my investigations. Some of these investigations hang close in my memory while some have drifted away. Without studying my files, I have the most memorable to tell about.

Now that I feel you have read what had influenced me most in my work, let me tell you about the *fun time*, the maybe not what others would call fun time, but what Jack Fleeman did and still appreciates the opportunity to have been involved. After all, this is, was, my dream!

Pickle Juice

I was the detective on-call one morning when I was called out to investigate an armed robbery at Burger King. It was about 6:30 in the morning and it seemed a bit unusual to have a robbery that early in the morning.

I headed that way and when I arrived, the uniformed officers had the restaurant secured on the outside and there were several night shift employees standing outside trying to get warm. It was quickly learned that several hours earlier, when the restaurant was closed, employees on the evening shift were emptying trash and cleaning up the business before they left work.

While the rear door was unlocked, while the trash was being taken out, three robbers entered the rear door, armed with a rifle. One of the robbers was a former employee, another was married to a former employee and the third robber was a guy with a long record. The robbers put the four employees into a cooler and locked them inside. After stealing the day's receipts, the robbers drained all the oil from the fryers, turned on all the gas jets, dumped paper trash in front of the cooler door and set it on fire as they fled. The robbers sped off, leaving clear tire markings in the asphalt at the rear door.

The day shift employees arrived a few hours later and found the rear door unlocked and the employees locked in the cooler. That is when police were called and then I arrived at the scene a short time later.

The oil was a mess on the floor, the gas had been shut off by arriving employees, but the pungent odor was still present as was the smell of smoke. I called the fire marshal to the scene since an arson had occurred and when he and I were examining the scene, we were scratching our heads as to how these people survived. The fire had burned significantly. We examined the burnt trash near the cooler and I found it was wet! No sprinkler system had been activated, so, what could have made the trash wet? I then smelled something familiar and picked up a piece of burned paper and smelled it. It was soaked with pickle juice. There had been a stainless-steel rack rolled near the cooler and it had a five-gallon plastic bucket of pickles on it. The heat from the fire melted the side of the bucket and the pickle juice drained out and extinguished the fire!

The place probably would have burned to the ground if it hadn't been for the pickle juice. A moment after this discovery, I just stared at the still-shivering victims who were gathered outside talking to officers. God had protected them.

I went on and investigated the case. I arrested all three robbers and they went to prison.

The Murder Cases

Probably the most memorable murder case involved a woman who was convicted of killing two of her children over a couple of year period. An ambulance was called to this woman's house early one morning to treat her baby who was unresponsive. She reported the baby was having seizures, and her pediatrician had given her previous instructions to give the baby a bath whenever the seizure occurred. The baby was pronounced dead at the Louisville hospital where it had been transported. The Kentucky coroner told our detectives that the case needed further investigation, possibly as a neglect case.

I wasn't involved directly in the case when it happened, but I knew investigators wanted to reinterview the mother. She had moved, and they couldn't find her.

I was working an unrelated investigation when I came across the mother by accident. She was staying with family members in a New Albany apartment. It had been several months since the baby had died, and I knew it was way past time for her to be brought back in. I had told Ron Kramer where she was staying, and he was in the process of lining up the child welfare investigators to assist him with another questioning. They had been checking out her story, and everything was appearing very suspicious. I think murder was far from their minds, but absolute neglect was on the forefront.

It was just a matter of days later before investigators had brought the woman in, when I overheard a terrible radio dispatch to Jeffersonville Police. I was due to go on duty in an hour or so, and I heard that a young child had been found dead in a bathtub in a housing project. An ambulance had taken the child to Clark Memorial Hospital in Jeffersonville and had been pronounced dead. I telephoned Ron Kramer, and I asked what he needed me to do. He told me that he and other detectives would be at the scene of the death, and he instructed me to go to the hospital and investigate from that point.

When I arrived at the emergency room, I was met with very solemn nurses who told me that a fourteen-month-old child had died. The mother of this child was the same mother involved in the other death. I knew right away what we were dealing with. We needed to find out the truth behind these children's deaths.

Of all of the death I have seen, the sight of that handsome fourteen-month-old child lying dead on a stretcher has stuck close in my mind. The attending nurse gave me the clothing the child was wearing when he was brought in. I had a problem distancing myself from the thought of my youngest child when I looked at this victim. It seemed not that long ago that Sara was that size, and I kept reminding myself to grow strong and take my feelings that were running strong within me and apply them to the strength I would need to investigate this. Both of these deaths were investigated. Within a day or so of the second death, a break came.

Late one afternoon, the manager of a local insurance office stopped by the detective office to see how the death of the second child was going to be ruled. It seemed the mother had just taken out an insurance policy on the child, and if the death was ruled accidental, she'd receive about forty thousand dollars.

It was soon after learning that when we discovered the first child that had died had a policy on it as well. The agent on that policy told us he had stopped by a short time before the death of the first child to see if this mother wanted to maintain the life insurance policy since her mother, the baby's grandmother, had been paying for it until she had died of an illness a short time earlier. This was the first time this mother knew about any insurance. She learned more than she bargained for with that agent's visit to her home. That visit would lead her to murder her own child.

Things had fallen into place very quickly, and we needed to act.

Enough evidence was gathered for the mother's arrest, and I was the chief investigator to testify at her trial. She was sentenced to a very long time in prison.

There was another murder that happened about a block from the police station. There were three men who had been drinking all day and had went to Louisville to the Kentucky State Fair. They became quite disruptive, and security officers escorted them out. They went back to Jeffersonville and continued their partying at an apartment. At some point, they began arguing after one of them started talking about having sex with underage girls. One of the men, at some point, retrieved a shotgun and shot that man. A neighbor had heard the shot but chose not to call police. It was about four hours later when police did get a call and found the scene. The dead guy was laying on the floor, and he had a knife in his hand. The other two guys said they shot him in self-defense. The problem was that the knife was in a bloodied hand, and no blood had been transferred to the knife. Those guys eventually told us the truth, including how they waited to call police to give them time to get a story together. They did admit they planted the knife. The dead guy had a reputation for being a bad person. The guy who did the shooting got probation and a suspended sentence. I never understood that. The neighbor who chose to ignore the sound of a shotgun was a known drug dealer. That I did understand.

There was this other case that always stayed with me. I knew the victim's sister, and I worked with a cousin of his. This group of people had somehow all gotten together at this girl's apartment and played cards all evening and basically just had a good time doing good, clean, honest things. At the latter part of the evening, the girl who lived at the apartment asked everyone to leave, as she needed to get to bed in order to work the following morning. One of the men who was there wasn't really close to any of them as he had recently gotten out of the service and was just having a good time. When they all left the girl's apartment, another man who lived next door invited the other guy to come to his apartment and watch television. That is what they did. The man who had gotten out of the service remarked at some point that he was tired, and the guy who lived there invited

135

him to sleep there and let him sleep in his bed. That apparently is where things went bad. The guy who lived there was gay, and the other guy awoke to find the gay guy performing oral sex on him. The gay guy was beaten to death in his own bed. To make things worse, the guy who killed him tried to even set the bed on fire.

The guy who did the killing ran several blocks to his sister's home and told her what had happened. In disbelief, she took her brother back to see for herself. They called the police after seeing a man had been killed.

While I was helping with the crime scene, I noticed a newspaper television schedule on a tabletop. I also noticed that the movie *The Burning Bed* had been on television that evening. It makes you wonder.

After several years as a detective, I eventually was sent back to uniform work. It was after a few days back on the street when I was dispatched to a shooting near downtown. This was shortly after six in the morning and very unusual. Upon arrival, I found a man shot to death lying near a tree. The man who shot him lived across the street from where the victim lay. I recovered the Intratek .9mm semiautomatic gun laying on the table inside the shooter's house. The shooter was known to have some mental issues and said the man who was shot had been tormenting him, and he shot him. The shooter went to prison. The place that sold him the gun got sued for selling him the gun.

I was somewhat familiar with the man who died. I had served a search warrant for drug dealing at a place he previously had lived. I never got to find out the truth about what the deal was when I searched his home. While searching, I found a chicken wire cage with baby toys in it. An informant told me that the man and his wife kept their child in the cage when they were partying.

The man who did the shooting was more familiar to me. I knew him to have some mental issues, and he lived at home with his mother. I knew his whole family. That was a tough one. He served his sentence. Today, as I write this, I see the gun daily on a shelf in the police department's evidence room. It's been there stored for the court since the court proceeding.

I can say that working homicides in Jeffersonville was always a challenge. I never worked a case where someone killed another person and just came in and admitted it saying, "Yeah, okay, I did it." Nor did I work a case where it was a clear-cut situation like an argument leading to a death leaving no question about the killer's identity.

I had this one case in a housing project where an argument over an early morning crap game out in the street led to a shooting. One guy held the victim down while his brother shot him.

I worked a killing where a woman killed the man she was drinking within his downtown apartment. He died upon arrival at the hospital. I went to the police station where she was being detained so I could question her. Yes, I suppose she did admit to this one, but when I told her that the man had died, she tore her shirt off and paraded all over the report room in plain view of a lady at the police station window who had no clue what had happened. Everything was a challenge, and I knew to grow from all of it. That was a secret of mine that I have never known any other officer I have worked with to take advantage of. I guess if they did, it was unknowingly.

I was involved with a few murders that remain unsolved. There was this one night the police station received a telephone call from a woman who told the dispatcher that Jack Fleeman needs to check on "so and so" (the victim). I was dispatched to the man's home in a housing project, knowing about the woman's call. I had no idea what to expect or why I needed to check on him. Upon arrival, I saw him through a window. He was dead. He had been shot twice in his chest.

One case I got involved with still leaves me wondering. The Jeff Police saw this guy swerving one night and pulled him over. There is a man driving and a man who is a front-seat passenger. While the officer is speaking to the driver to determine if he is drunk or whatever, another officer arrives as a backup. The second officers see that the passenger has his hand on a gun and things get wild for a few moments and the passenger was arrested. The driver had been kidnapped and was being forced to drive from ATM to ATM to withdraw cash for the kidnapper. The driver swerved intentionally, hoping he'd get stopped by the police officer.

While this *bad guy* is being taken to jail, he brags that if the police think they have something here, call a homicide detective, and he'll really get things rolling. We did, and he did. He drew a map along the city's riverfront to a body. The victim had been shot and left along the bank of the Ohio River. The killer told us how he and the victim had been there drinking, and he shot him for no reason. We found records where we responded to reports of a gunshot a couple of nights earlier. The killer went to jail, and after a stint in a mental hospital, it was determined he was fit to plead guilty and go to prison.

This same guy had been released not that long ago from another prison. When he was due to be released from that prison, he sent the president of the United States a threatening letter and got another five years to spend there. This guy had 666 engraved on his forehead. We found satanic altars in a storage building where he had been hired to do some work, and we found a similar altar near where we found the murder victim along the riverbank.

After going to prison, he sent one of the detectives a letter telling where he had a couple of more victims buried along the riverbank. We arranged for one of the nation's best cadaver dogs and its handler, a Massachusetts State Trooper, to be flown in to perform a search. The trooper was a member of the FBI's Evidence Recovery Team. We never found any more bodies, but we did not dismiss the killer's claims. The dog as well as another cadaver dog from the FBI hit on a location twice over a full one-year period. There were so many factors about what the rise and fall of river levels could affect any evidence left behind, and the same for considering animals that live along the banks that I learned there were probably many factors working against us when we searched the area. The public was kept out of it. We had heavy equipment brought down to the river, built earthen dams, drained the area, and did whatever we could without actually disturbing the river area. It was a great learning experience.

When the killer sent this letter, he told us that after we found the two bodies there, he'd tell us about eleven women he had killed. FBI profilers studied the letter and felt assured we may very well have a couple of more victims, but it was felt the killer was pulling our chain about those women victims.

I had experienced using a cadaver dog before. We had this couple show up at the police station about midnight one time and told us that they witnessed a man being killed several days earlier, and that the victim had been buried inside a garage a few blocks from police headquarters.

This guy, who dressed like a woman, had argued with his male friend at the killer's home over another man. The cross-dressing guy stabbed his soon-to-be ex-dead boyfriend, and the victim ran across the street and died in a city park. They stored his corpse in the trunk of a car in front of the house for a couple of days while they tried to figure out where to dispose of it. They finally chose the garage. It was owned by a relative of the killer. The woman who owned the garage gave me permission to take a look. I broke a padlock off the door and sure enough, I found a fresh grave on the dirt floor of the garage. That was about one in the morning.

At daybreak, we executed a search warrant on the garage. We conducted what you could compare to an archeological dig to carefully recover the body. We determined the body was in fact there, and at that moment, our SWAT team raided the house where the killer and some others were located.

That killer went to prison. I had heard a rumor that he married another man since he has been there.

We later called in a cadaver dog from the Kentucky State Police to give the area a thorough search. The dog, Bingo, did a good job. He hit hard on the garage where we had already recovered the victim, but with Bingo's help, we were satisfied there were no other victims in the area.

My Career is Winding Down

My career went on for several more years. Most memories seem to be of the bad times. Countless deaths, violent crimes, jury trials, and heavy workloads seem to be the main source of memories.

As I got older, I was promoted and began becoming more and more of a supervisor. The significance of a crime seemed overshadowed by manpower shortages, long hours, and frustrations associated with my concerns of getting the job done as compared to being the one doing the actual job.

I was working with guys who seemed to enjoy the power and prestige of rank. That was fine. We all had different upbringings, experiences, training, goals, and lives. It just didn't seem to jibe with my priorities.

The last thirteen years of my career were served as I held the rank of major. This was within the detective division, and then the uniform division. I think my age, experiences, and general frustrations with being an administrator of sorts led to my decision one day to approach the chief of police and ask for a transfer to another position. I was offered a chance to take over the evidence room, and I immediately accepted the offer.

I worked as the administrator of the evidence room for the final five years of my career. I took over the reins of an evidence room that was extremely too small, and I was involved in a process of converting an indoor pistol range within the courthouse into an evidence room. The area was cleaned of lead hazards, and several hundred thousand pieces of evidence were transferred into the new storage facility. The job seemed to fit me fine.

I maintained control of chain of evidence, disposed of old evidence, updated files, transferred evidence to a variety of forensic labs, and continued to testify in court.

Then one day, it happened. I had been thinking about retirement, and one thing happened that pushed me to make the decision to retire. Another police officer showed up at the evidence room door. He had just returned from sick leave and was placed on light duty in the evidence room to assist me. This officer seemed like this might be his last stop. He had trained me for the evidence room and now had returned with a possible long-lasting physical recovery.

I went to the chief of police and discussed possibly retiring. I decided to retire in a few months.

This gave me ample time to set up a business I had long contemplated. I became owner of Fleeman Investigations, Inc. And in June 2010, my retirement was official.

I had a huge retirement party. Music, food, and a few hundred guests certainly made a great send-off for me. I received great comments on my behalf from former mayors and police officers. The Secret Service awarded me with a plaque recognizing my career and assistance to them, and the Fraternal Order of Police presented me with an award. The presenter, Joe Hubbard, made a personal comment of something he appreciated about working with me over many years. Joe told the crowd that he never went on a run with me when I didn't make a point to explaining to other officers what we did, why we did it, and what we could expect if something didn't work out.

It's just like I mentioned early in this book. We all have to learn from everything we do.

About the Author

The author served as a police officer for over thirty-six (36) years. The majority of the time he served as a detective. Since retiring in 2010, he has owned his own private investigation firm and lives and works in Southern Indiana in the Louisville, Kentucky, area.

CPSIA information can be obtained
at www.ICGtesting.com
Printed in the USA
BVHW031525301121
622853BV00001B/10